One Foot in the Grave, the Other Groping for Life

Lessons for Christians' and Christianity's Survival in the Twenty-First Century

Yvonne Ardoin Dardeau

ISBN 978-1-63630-449-6 (Paperback)
ISBN 978-1-63630-450-2 (Digital)

Covenant Books, Inc.
11661 Hwy 707
Murrells Inlet, SC 29576
www.covenantbooks.com

I dedicate this work to Mary Alice Fontenot and Susan Lahaye for their decades of loving friendship and support, through "thick and thin". I could not have been so "sane" without you. Thank you.

Introduction

CHRISTIANITY, THE RELIGION established by Jesus, the Son of God, is the religion that enlightened the world to the knowledge that God wanted to share his glory; he created mankind out of his love. God is love, and each of us was created by God in love to share his glory.

This book is a collection of lessons centered around a truth of Christianity that we Christians need to learn and practice so that we and our Christian culture can survive this twenty-first-century environment. The culture worldwide is not only intolerant but hostile toward the one God and toward religion, especially Christianity, and especially faithful Christians. This intolerance is sometimes subtle but often verbally and physically abusive.

This attack on Christianity is not a new phenomenon, but it has been aggressive and threatening in this century; sadly, Christians' reactions have been weak at best but more often have been silent and unresponsive. The world, ruled by the devil, has always been an enemy of God. This is shown throughout the Holy Bible, beginning with Adam and Eve and continuing after the birth, death, resurrection of Jesus and the establishment of his religion, Christianity. The book of Wisdom describes vividly the reasons why the world, in the past and today, hates those of us who follow Jesus as teacher, Lord, and Savior. They hate those of us who follow Jesus's teachings and the commandments of God. Wisdom 2:12–22 states that we are obnoxious to the liberal worldly groups who see in our behavior, our words, and sometimes our silence a judgement on their way of life. Our way of life, often radically opposed to the worldly, serves as a constant reminder of our disapproval of their values and morals. This is intolerant to many anti-Christians who want us not only to tolerate but to accept and agree with that which we know is evil: abortion and some sinful, inappropriate sexual behaviors are primary issues of friction. We must no longer remain silent or inactive. Not only are our bodies in danger of destruction today, as with the current pandemic, but our souls are in danger too because we Christians have not lived our lives according to the purpose for which God created us: to know, love, serve, and obey him. In our culture, we have not followed his will.

These forty lessons in forty chapters to be read for forty days in this book are like the forty days Jesus spent praying and fasting in the desert before he began his public teaching of the arrival of the kingdom of God. We will spend our forty days studying some of our Christian beliefs based on the teachings of Jesus. He has told us in John 14:6 that he is the "way, the truth, the life"; we follow him to align ourselves and our culture with his teachings. We will learn, relearn, review, and recommit ourselves; we, the whole world, are in crisis, even before the current pandemic. Well-lived Christianity is key to the planet's well-being; therefore, we are very much needed.

How are we to survive the chaotic times and remain faithful to God through Jesus, who loves us? What actions are we to take to help our culture become Christian again? God has a plan right now for each of us to protect and to save our world, even now with this new threat, the pandemic. Perhaps we are needed now more than ever before.

Jerimiah 1:5 tells us that God created us in our mothers' wombs. He formed us just as he wanted us. And he placed us here and now, in this place and in this time of the twenty-first century. He knew the battles we would have against the world, the devil, and our own weaknesses. He knew the obstacles; he provided us with all we would need to be victorious. With him, we will gain the final victory, fulfilling the purposes for which he created us.

Each lesson is some teaching of our Christian faith, Jesus's religion, focusing on the purpose for which we were born. Ideas, insights, and guides are explored to help us understand and practice a truth about the purpose for which God made us. Each lesson is independent, complete. The common bond of the chapters is the theme: knowing, loving, and serving God by following Jesus, his church, and his religion, Christianity. There are suggested resolutions at the end of each lesson designed to aid our journey. The Scripture passages cited, and the passages before and after these quotes, can be helpful to understanding the lessons and provide study and familiarity with the Bible.

Nothing presented is new; the truths of God's love and his goal for our lives never change. Therefore, we need to review and study these truths, month after month, year after year, until death, because we will never be finished learning and understanding the things of God while we are here on earth. No time in recent history has the whole world been on its knees before an invisible, foreign enemy, a virus; no time in recent history have we Christians needed to turn our thoughts, our prayers, and our lives to God, whom we have neglected, the one whom we have refused to obey, the one whom we have refused to depend on. We twenty-first Christians, like most of the Western world, believe that we do not need God, that we could be independent of him. We need to work at changing this culture; but first, we must change our minds, attitudes, and then our actions. Lord, have mercy and help us!

Chapter 1

Fear Not the Battle

CHRISTIANS, IN THESE times of anger, chaos, confusion, and much fear, we must learn to "be not afraid" as Jesus so often tells us in the gospels, as we find in Matthew 14:7 and Matthew 28:10. The enemy, Satan and his world in which we live, is powerful. But Jesus is the general, the leader of his army, us Christians. True, we can lose our physical lives now, but we will not lose our immortal souls if we follow him. Meanwhile, we must *put aside our fears* and *act* as warriors for the salvation of our souls, the souls of our loved ones, and for the survival of our Christian world. We must ignore our fears and confusion, especially now in this "war" in which the pandemic has overwhelmed us. As Saint Padre Pio tells us, "It is necessary to be strong... that is our duty. Life is a struggle which we cannot avoid. We must triumph!"

What are the symptoms, the causes, the remedies of this war, which we Christian warriors must know so that we can effectively "do battle" for Christ and for ourselves?

Religion, especially Christianity, is viewed with animosity, distaste, and suspicion by many of our contemporaries. Many people blame us Christians for divisions in society; they claim that we keep society from needed changes in beliefs, values, and morals. The world considers Christianity to be irrelevant, obsolete, and dangerous because Christians prevent "progress" in people's rights; Christianity is committed to the laws of God, the laws of nature, and

Jesus's teachings instead of society's "changeable" democratic laws and opinions.

Every century has had its spiritual battles, sometimes ending in actual physical wars. One aspect of the enemy fighting against Christianity in this century seems to be one of attitudes: apathy, indifference, and disbelief in God and Jesus. It appears that Christianity is losing many skirmishes because many Christians are ignorant of the battle raging for our hearts, minds, and souls; and too many of us are ignorant of the teachings of our Christian faith.

For example, our lack of knowledge of Scripture, Jesus's teachings, and our own Christian beliefs and teachings has made us vulnerable to the devil's tactics. We do not know how to refute or understand the "false and distorted" facts given by the world. We then often believe that which is not true. This makes us weak and ineffective against the demon's attacks in our world.

And we Christians have been lazy and self-satisfied, filled with the pleasures that the world (our enemy) offers. Christian morals and values are disappearing. In Philippians 3:19, Saint Paul warns us, as he did the Philippians, of the severe consequences of our lifestyles, which, like theirs, seem to have our belly (sensual pleasures) as our god; and we honor our shameful behavior. We honor the sins of the world with celebrations and parades; we raise our voices in acceptances of that which is totally unacceptable in the eyes of God.

Therefore, all Christians, arise! We must awake from our comfortable slumber to fully grasp the reality of the threats to our Christian way of life; perhaps the present pandemic has or will awaken some of us. Our Christian world is under powerful attack. This "awakening" to this reality is a necessary first step in becoming a warrior for Christianity.

Each one of us is called upon to join in Jesus Christ's fighting army; we must be part of the solution. How? Spiritual battles have always been won by those Christians who first won their own interior battles. We Christians must be prepared for the battle of our lifetime by achieving personal holiness through deep conversions.

And so as we begin in earnest the process of becoming the warrior that Christianity needs in this world, we need to believe, as our own truth, that God loves us and that he created us because of this love. God placed us here to work in his world here and now. We love and serve God by working and serving him in our neighbor; we are responsible to work at keeping God's world out of the devil's hands. We must struggle; we cannot afford to be lazy and indifferent. We cannot say, "There is nothing I can do."

The first and best weapon that we all, no matter our age or circumstance, can use is prayer. *The power of prayer is not being utilized; much prayer, by individuals, groups, nations, is the first and foremost answer to all the problems encountered by us personally and in our culture.* Without prayer, asking for God's mercy and forgiveness and help, action is useless. Sharing in established prayer groups and establishing new groups, groups for study of Scripture and Christian formation, are within the reach of most of us Christian; these groups are necessary and of great value to the army fighting the devil and the world's attacks. Many groups of Christians, usually affiliated with a church, can provide the praise and honor due to God; and groups can gather knowledge and understanding of our faith. This knowledge and understanding are vital weapons to use against devilish propaganda against Christians. Prayer, study groups, and prayer groups will be vital to combat the enormous army of devils, who are helped by the multitudes of naive, ignorant Christians who have no idea they are serving Satan!

One-by-one, we Christians will defeat the enemies of Christ and the enemies of our poor world when we courageously push our fears aside and do the work required of us. This work is not easy, but Christians' indifference, laziness, and selfishness have contributed greatly to the present chaotic time. Now it is our responsibility to help stop the slide. The Christian and his world have one foot in the grave of destruction of his Christian culture, and the other foot is groping for life by kicking at the devil's attacks, like the virus. It will take much work to keep this world from sliding into the pit. As

Saint Paul tells us in Philippians 4:13, we can do all things through the strength of Christ, who will help us.

1. In what ways can I prepare myself to be a better warrior for Christ? (Join or start a prayer or study group? Make a retreat? Join a lay community?)
2. What plans will I make?
3. I will read Bible passages to learn more about Jesus and Christianity.

Notes: I will write ideas, plans, and questions to keep for review and reference.

Chapter 2

Guiding Principle for All Christians

WHAT IS THE principle that people have as their focus, the *guiding star* of their lives, their goal of life? Christians have always had directions and principles, focus, to base their lives on. Not all of us know, care, or follow this principle. First, it was the Old Testament teachings from the Jewish religion. Then it was Jesus himself. Next, it was the apostles' teachings, the early church, the church fathers. Eventually, we had the New Testament. Today, we have additional guidance from two other sources to help us clarify and summarize the guiding principle into clear direction. This principle can and should help us to know and understand what God wants us to have as the goal of our lives; it clarifies why God created us.

One principle that guides Christians was given by the influential spiritual leader Ignatius of Loyola; he lived from 1491 to 1556, but his principles are still very much in use. Ignatius's first principle states that *man is created to "praise, reverence, and serve God."* In other words, Ignatius tells us why God created us: to praise, revere, and serve God. The principle continues this way: *everything in the world is created to help man achieve the goal of his creation, and anything that obstructs this goal must be given up.* Therefore, according to Ignatius, our lives should focus on the ways that help us to achieve this principle: praising, revering, and serving him. And we must avoid anything and anyone that keeps us from this goal.

Then, we have a second clear source, *The Baltimore Catechism,* the book that educated generations of Catholics and many other Christians from 1885 to 1960. One of the first, if not the first, questions in the original book was, "Why did God create me?" The answer given was, "God created me to know Him, to love Him, to serve Him, and to be happy with Him forever in heaven."

These two sources, which have been followed by Christians for centuries, in fact, state the same principle. This is the basic, rock-bottom principle that we Christians should follow as a guide for our entire lives. Many spiritual leaders of all Christian denominations have taught us this important principle, this ideal; they have helped us to know how to fulfill this goal. They have taught us that being happy with God begins here on earth as we grow in holiness on our spiritual journey back to God in heaven.

This task, fulfilling this principle, is difficult. However, God is not only good and merciful; he is also logical. He has given us a task, the purpose of our creation, which he knows we can achieve because he will help us. Besides, in creating us, he made sure that we had all we needed to accomplish this. Then Jesus, truly God and truly Man, came to teach us by his life and his teachings how to fulfill the purpose of our lives.

In simple language and terms, how do we achieve this?

In Matthew 14:27–31, we have the story of Peter, who was so excited to see Jesus walking on the water that he asked Jesus to let him, Peter, do it. Jesus said, "Come." Peter began walking on the water; he began to look at the waves, feel the strong winds. Peter began to sink because he looked away from Jesus. Yes, we must keep our eyes on Jesus, no matter the conditions we are in. Our problems, troubles—the evil in the world can distract us from focusing on Jesus. We must lean on Jesus, trusting that God, who loves us, is taking care of everything. All that comes to us—that which we like or dislike, that which brings joy, and that which brings sorrow—all is from God, or it happens with his permission. Even the beauty and pleasures of this world must not become more important than God. Loved ones must not distract us from our life's purpose, although they are all gifts from God.

Also, we must give our hearts to Jesus. We must *know* Jesus personally if we are to love him. We cannot love anyone whom we do not know. Therefore, to stay focused on our life's purpose, knowing and loving Jesus is not optional. To do this, we spend *our whole lives* meditating on the life of Jesus and getting to know him as a person. We meditate on Jesus's coming to this earth and why; we think of how he spent thirty years of poverty and hard work to teach us what matters most in life. We meditate on Jesus's three years of teaching and preaching to tell us about the Father's love and mercy, performing great miracles to authenticate his divinity. We meditate on the mystery of Jesus suffering torture and crucifixion to open the gates of heaven for us. Then he arose from the dead to further prove his divinity and to establish his religion, Christianity.

Yes, we must internalize the truth that God created us to know, love, and serve him and to be happy with him forever. We must focus on the truth that we must follow Jesus, the Son of God, our Savior, our brother, and our teacher. Then we will be fulfilling the duty that God wants and needs from us. The reason for our creation will be met. Our God will be pleased. He might say of us what he said of Jesus in Luke 9:35: "This is my beloved son."

1. How often do I meditate on the purpose for which God created me?
2. Now that I really know this, what will I do differently?

Notes:

Chapter 3

Acedia: The Great
Evil of Our Time

THE DEMON *ACEDIA*, well-known in ages past, had been forgotten for centuries. It has recently been reintroduced by Christian church leaders and theologians. Probably the main reason for it getting renewed attention is that our present culture, universally, has become known for its apathy and indifference toward God and religion; this is true even for those of us who are baptized Christians. This has been called the great evil of our century. The demon acedia is the name of the devil who is blamed for this evil, the greatest problem for twenty-first-century Christianity.

A good, clear introduction for acedia is given in a book review of *The Noonday Devil: Acedia, the Unnamed Evil of Our Times*, written by Jean-Charles Nault, abbot of Saint-Wandrille, Normandy, France. The reviewer is American Cardinal Marc Ouelle, prefect of the Congregation for Bishops. Cardinal Ouelle writes, "'The noonday devil' is demon of acedia, the vice is also known as sloth. The word "sloth," however, can be misleading, for acedia is not laziness; in fact it can manifest as busyness or activism. Rather, acedia is a gloomy combination of weariness, sadness, and a lack of purposefulness. It robs a person of his capacity for joy and leaves him feeling empty, or void of meaning. Although its name hearkens back to antiquity and the Middle Ages, and seems to have been largely forgotten, acedia is experienced by countless modern people who describe their condition as depression, melancholy, burn-out, or even mid-life crisis." The word refers to both the name of the demon and the condition.

Evagrius of Pontus, who lived in AD 345–399, wrote about acedia in discussing the Desert Fathers; they were monks who left the world, including other monks, fleeing to the desert for isolation, in order to pray and fast. Evagrius wrote of the monks' temptation by acedia. He described the great temptation that occurred between 10:00 a.m. and 2:00 p.m. when the barren desert was at the hottest time of the day and at the time that the monks were most tempted to seek company, to seek companionship, to run away from their vocation. Evagrius named the devil acedia the "noonday devil" because it was the time of the most violent temptations; the hot and tired monks were at their most vulnerable at this time.

The symptoms of acedia are common and familiar for us today, although the cause is mostly unknown. Acedia is difficult to define because there are so many different manifestations caused by this devil. Throughout the centuries, acedia (the demon) has been defined as despair, boredom, laziness, carelessness, and indifference. Evagrius, when giving the symptoms that affected the monks, defined symptoms that are clearly visible in our time. He said that the monks were tempted to move, to change vocations because they were bored, frustrated, exhausted; they were easy prey for the devil unless they were strongly committed to their vocation, which God had willed for them. This condition describes millions of us today. This malady may account for millions of prescriptions for depression and anxiety. It could account for the many suicides, especially among young people. Acedia has successfully targeted workplaces, social and government institutions, religions, marriages, and families, causing divisions, abuses, destructions.

The monks had to struggle to strengthen the virtues that made it possible to "stay the course," although tempted to change to somewhere or something or someone different. We all sometimes feel that "the grass is greener on the other side." Everything that Evagrius described for the monks, we modern Christian experience. We too must struggle to know, love, serve God and others in the place that God has placed us.

There are temptations today that the monks did not have that we Christians must avoid as faithful Christians. Our modern world tempts us with many pleasures that can totally distract us from the duties of our vocation: social media, television, movies. Many people who live immoral ways of life but are "good human people" can beguile and confuse us; mind-altering drugs, alcohol, food and drink that dull our rational minds while feeding our senses, and a great many other temptations are available for acedia to use in tempting us. The devil knows our peculiar weaknesses; that is one reason why we must be on constant guard to preserve our Christian life.

The world tempts us with the false attitudes that the monks might have not encountered. Our world tells us that we are entitled to all the comforts and pleasures that we desire; the world tells us that following Jesus's teachings is too difficult, is no longer valid in our modern world. The demon acedia has so many tools to use against us.

The answer to the temptations of acedia for us is the same as it was for the monks who lived in the desert centuries ago. We must struggle daily to remain in "our place," which is what God, our loving Father, has chosen for us. We are often tempted, tired of struggling, bored, and stressed. Fighting against the temptations are the crosses, the hardships of our spiritual journeys. God made us to know, love, and serve him and be happy with him forever now and in eternity. We achieve this with patient perseverance in the place where we are.

1. I will think about my temptations from the demon acedia; I will make plans to fight these.
2. I will rise quickly after I fall in fulfilling God's will for me; this is a good way to defeat acedia.
3. I will pray more fervently when I fall.

Notes:

Chapter 4

Babbling Adults

WE ARE ALL familiar with the babbling of babies, especially when they first find that they have a voice; it so delightful. The babbling of adults, making no sense to us, is not a delight but an irritation and a cause of much trouble and chaos.

In Genesis 11:1–9, the story of the Tower of Babel illustrates the growing evil of the people of ancient Babylonia. The Babylonians decided to build themselves a city with its tower reaching to the heavens, making themselves famous for creating their own path to heaven. They were a proud, independent people, all speaking the same language. They believed that they had no need of God. God intervened! He scrambled their language into many languages; they no longer understood each other. Now, the speech of one group sounded like "babbling" to the other groups. They scattered throughout the world; tribes with the same languages formed new tribes and new enemies.

Wow! That is our story too! Any news on any media source shows the reality of the fact that *division reigns; there is much babbling of different groups directed at the members of the "other tribe, group, party, nation."* This is our situation now as in Babylonian time: the devil's works of anger, chaos, hatred, violence are prevalent.

There are several influential groups in our culture today. The belief systems of these groups are not always strictly adhered to; the lines get blurred. But in general, there are sharply different beliefs, value systems, morals, even lifestyles. We need to understand the differences in and similarities of the groups and our own place in these groups. We need to understand what must be done so that the chaos and hatred and violence stop; we need to know our responsibilities to help bring calm in this babbling culture.

One group, often called the conservative Christian group, is the group that has most members trying very seriously to follow the commandments of God, the teachings of Jesus, his church, and his religion, Christianity. Those of us in this group are faithful in attending church services, in participating in the financial support of the church, and in activities for our spiritual growth. We actively support pro-Christian laws and way of life. We pray, meditate, read Christian spiritual books and use Christian media sites for information, encouragement, and inspiration. We are the flock of Christians that the culture often treats harshly and abusively in words and deeds.

Another group of us baptized Christians are called liberal Christians. We often attend church services and participate in the activities of the church and even its financial support. We follow many of the commandments of God, the teachings of Jesus and the church. However, we are of the strong opinion that we have the right to follow the teachings, laws, and rules of which we approve, and that we can choose to ignore those of which we disapprove. It appears that many Christians are in this flock.

However, many of us baptized, nonpracticing Christians partially follow the Christian way of the New Testament. And many non-Christians too partially follow the Christian way of the New Testament. The New Testament is especially concerned with love of neighbor and the peaceful ways to live, which is ordered by love, justice, kindness, goodness, respect for all people. Many nonpracticing Christians and non-Christians know that this way of life is the most effective way to live and to preserve society. (It was practicing Christians who converted the pagan Roman Empire, and they also converted other pagan societies. Practicing Christians converted pagan societies primarily through the love they showed, not only for their fellow Christians, but for all people.)

Today, the fastest-growing group in our Western culture is non-Christian people. This group of people is often at least second and third generations of nonpracticing Christians; they are far removed from the influence of the Holy Scripture, God's commandments, and Jesus's teachings. They have little or no relationship with the Christian God and Jesus of the Holy Scripture. They are not influenced by the tenets of Christianity. They have been educated by the "world," the devil's playground. As this number grows, the Christian influence declines; the godless, loveless pagan numbers grow.

People in this group generally have no *order, internally in their thinking and attitudes and outwardly in their behavior; there is little respect for authority, rules, and laws.* There are too many people who have no foundation of life based on the teachings of the Old and New Testament and Jesus's teachings, which show the value of knowing and obeying these teachings. The result is that chaos, anger, hatred of the "other" group rises. This is what the culture is experiencing now.

The babbling goes on. Christians "babble" to groups who see us as irrelevant, hypocritical, angry, joyless people. Some of us are. Many view Christians as "talkers of the way of Jesus," but they observe that "we do not walk the way that we claim he walked." They do not see Jesus reflected in us! They do not listen to us; they believe that we are babbling nonsense. Many non-Christians and nonpracticing Christians babble worldly reasoning, scientific jargon, and New Age spiritual language, which are not related to Jesus's teachings.

What are we to do to calm our chaotic world? We Christians know the answer. The discordant babbling between groups in the world, even in our Christian societies, will stop only when all societies again speak the love language of God, of Jesus Christ.

How will this be accomplished? We Christians must take strong, rational, purposeful actions. We must convince our present world that Jesus is the answer; we must evangelize, not half-heartedly, but strongly, as our forefathers did in other centuries. We must preach and live the whole truth; only partially following Jesus is not good enough!

How? Only *by our own deep conversions first will this happen.* Only by our own *Christian examples, actions, way of life* will non-Christians and nonpracticing Christians be interested in hearing our language as rational and worthwhile. We must be strong, courageous, but respectful in living our Christian way of life. And we must be able to recognize the dangerous opposition to Christianity, and we must challenge this opposition whenever it is appropriate to do so.

We ourselves must be first conquered by and for God through Jesus. This is our task, our duty. There is no time to waste. The small, invisible virus that is plaguing the world now is telling us to "wake up" and start now the true, deep conversion. Nothing else will do. The angry babbling between groups in the world, even in our Christian societies, will change only when all people speak the love language of God, of Jesus Christ.

1. I will examine my conscience to recognize the areas where I must improve, be converted. I will continue to make plans to know and love God through Jesus.

2. I will pray fervently to the Holy Spirit to help me "wake up" and follow my plans.

Notes:

Chapter 5

Living Life on Two Levels

DO WE WORK to earn a living; to take care of our families and ourselves; to have money for a new car, a vacation; to add to our savings for emergencies and retirement and other such reasons, even working because we love what we are doing? Are we living a life without formal work, retired because of age or other good circumstances, or are we disabled and still fulfilling all duties for which we are responsible and capable of doing? These are all good, natural activities that we do in our daily lives to make our lives and the lives of others around us peaceful and secure.

Do we try not to harm anyone and do good to others where and when we can? Do we try to live patiently and quietly with the troubles, problems, tragedies, and sufferings that happen to all of us? All these are good, natural human activities that benefit the whole world; these are duties assigned by God to each of us.

Now, let us consciously and deliberately place our daily life in the kingdom of God. We know that God created us to know, love, and serve him so that we can live happily with him forever. And we know that we fulfill this command by doing our duties here, where we are placed, the vocations, the families, the environment that God provided for us. Therefore, the duties that we must or should be doing well should be done for two reasons. We do the duties of our life to have a successful, peaceful earthly life, which is beneficial not only for ourselves but also for the world around us. Another reason, whether we realize it or not, is to benefit our eternal life after this earthly life is finished and God calls us home.

The rewards of our eternal life will be those we have earned from our birth until our last breath; we can do nothing more after this to increase our rewards. Therefore, as the old saying states, "We need to make hay while the sun shines."

How do we do this? God is good and merciful and just. He knows what each of us can do with his help and support, so he does not expect more than what our present life offers. We can accumulate incredible wealth for our eternal life and for the lives of others right here, right now. We do this by being conscious of our supernatural goal: to know, love, and serve God. All our daily activities can be "supernaturalized" by offering each activity to God. Many of us offer God our "prayers, works, joys, and sufferings of this day" in making a morning offering prayer. Many of us promptly forget this and go on with our busy, difficult, happy, and sorrowful day without thinking of God again. And often, this happens because of unusual happenings and circumstances in our day, but most often it is because we have not trained ourselves to do more. We have not acquired the habit of silently, quietly, and simply offering up to God every activity, duty, happening, work, problem as they occur.

How is this done? It is not difficult; it is saying prayers before or during anything or any event in our day. Some examples of this simple method of supernatural elevation of our thoughts are "God, bless our visit"; "God, I offer you this chore which I detest"; "God, bless this painful illness I am suffering"; "God, help me"; "God, I am afraid, nervous, confused"; "I need help."

Then, we are living in the present moment with God our entire days, our entire lives. We do not have to live in monasteries; we live in our busy daily lives here and now. We pray for help in making decisions, in solving problems, in our boredom, and in the joyful events. And we pray this way for others. We ask for their needs. God hears us! And we will be fulfilling Jesus's command, as told in Luke 18:1, "Pray always."

There may be a serious problem. What if we have activity or lifestyle that we know is wrong, sinful? We must stop this now; if we cannot stop but we want to or do not know how to change this situation, we need to ask for help. First, and always, we ask God to help us find a solution. We ask God often, begging! We might try getting guidance from our pastors or some trustworthy Christian friend or counselor. Meanwhile, we give to God our good deeds for his glory, for the remission of sins. *When we are sincere, God does step in and give us his help. But we must be patient; God's time is not our time. It can be in days, weeks, years before God answers.*

Leading a double life usually means a false, often sinful, life, in secret from others around us, while pretending that the life they see is the "real" thing. *But living a supernatural life along with our natural life, offering to God everything we do, is the "real" thing. And it is simple, it is beautiful, it carries us into eternity. Glory to God!*

1. I will try to remember to supernaturalize my life starting today.
2. I will fail to remember. I will start again; falling and rising again is pleasing to God.

Notes:

Chapter 6

Beware the Hazards in Our Spiritual Journey

MANY OF US Christians, sometimes occasionally, sometimes often, desire to be more faithful Christians; we want to know and follow Jesus more closely. We may sometimes want to know, love, and serve God better. We may realize that we are not serving him as we should, and that we do not know how to serve him. These thoughts are inspirations from the Holy Spirit, urging us to do the "something more" we are desiring. The Holy Spirit is prodding us to be a more faithful, loving disciple of Jesus.

If we Christians would continue in our exuberance after the Holy Spirit has awakened us at various times during retreats, conferences, Christian rallies, our pastors' words and sermons, there would be a holy change in us, in our environment. The Holy Spirit would take our joyful beginning, help the growth in our desire to be more faithful to God through Jesus, and give us many opportunities to develop this desire. Why is it that we do nothing, or that we attempt to do something and then quit?

Why is it that so many of us do not "stay" and deepen our relationship and love of Jesus? The rich young man in the parable of Mark 10:17–31 tells us one reason why we quit. When the rich young man asked Jesus what he had to do to become closer to God, Jesus's answer frightened him. He was told that he had to sell his riches and come follow Jesus. The gospel writer tells us that the young man loved his riches too much, but he turned away sad. Jesus was sad too, for Jesus loved him. Most of us are not asked to give up our riches to follow Jesus, unless we are acquiring them in sinful, evil ways; nor do we usually have to give up important gifts that God has given us, including family. Usually, these gifts do not interfere with following Jesus; if they do interfere in a consistent way, we may have to make changes after much prayer, support, and counseling from strong Christians and our church. Therefore, *to love something or someone more than Jesus is one reason why we do not continue to convert our lives more fervently to Jesus.*

Another reason why we may not continue in learning to know and love Jesus more is that we may have serious sins that we do not want to give up. We love our sin too much; we do not want to change. (Sometimes our sinful life involves someone else, which complicates things for us. Christian counseling by strong Christians can be a great help in these sensitive areas.)

Too often, the joy of the new interest in Jesus, in God, fizzles; and we soon return to our "blah-blah-blah" condition. Why? *An important reason is that after these encounters when we are "touched by God," we have no means of continuing the experience.* On our own, like infants learning to walk, we fall back to our old place in our spiritual life because we do not have the support, the enthusiasm of others to help us. In our baby steps, we need others to hold our hand, to pick us up when we fall, to help us in dangerous situations. We need a support system. If we do not have one, *we must seek for that help and support; it is our responsibility.* We must ask Jesus to send us his Holy Spirit to help us find this help and support. Sometimes it requires a great deal of searching. We must not give up. Jesus says, as recorded in Matthew7:7, seek and you will find that which you are looking for.

An important reason why we Christians abandon our spiritual journey to and with Jesus is that we fear the narrow road that Jesus talks about. In Matthew 17:13–14, Jesus warns us that the way to God, heaven, is narrow, indicating difficulties for us. In other words, we are afraid to suffer unnecessarily, believing that we suffer more of the ordinary sufferings that all of us must endure in this life. We do not understand that suffering, well accepted and borne, is asked of all people, Christian or not. The reason for suffering is Adam's sin of disobedience, which brought suffering and death in the world.

Sidestepping the hazardous thinking, and accompanied by Jesus, we can walk the spiritual road toward God, following in the footsteps of Jesus, who continuously turns to us with help and support. We do this in sickness and good health, in suffering and pain, and in consolations and joy because we know that we are on the right path with Jesus.

1. Am I on the road that leads to God with Jesus?
2. What do I need to change if I am going the wrong way? Do I want to change?
3. I will study Scripture passages.

Notes:

Chapter 7

Protective Brotherly Love

IN ANCIENT DAYS, cities were fortified by walls built all around them, with guards patrolling day and night, watching for enemies who would come into a weak spot in the wall and destroy all within. Unfortified, unprotected cities were often overrun by their enemies.

In Proverbs 18:19, we learn that a brother is a better defense than a strong city, and a friend is like the bars of a castle. Love and care from brothers and friends are compared to the strong defenses of ancient cities. This is an indication of how important it is to be a strong defense for someone and to have someone who is a strong defense for us. How is this done? Who needs our love and care? What characteristics must we possess so that we are strong walls for others?

When we help others, we provide them with invaluable gifts. We may provide needed material goods and physical assistance when it is appropriate, and when it is within our ability to do so. But there is also help that requires a more personal, even intimate, support, and that is verbal or nonverbal signals that indicate that we care about them. We give others signals that we understand their situation, that we stand behind and for them in their need. This requires, often, continual reaching out, personally or by telephone calls, messages, e-mails.

When we help other people, we provide the needed strength, support, and protection from what is weakening them. And the reverse is also true; we need the same when we face problems. Whenever we are struggling with illness, loneliness, physical or mental or spiritual needs, we are extremely fortunate if others, be they one person or more, come to our assistance. Not feeling alone in our troubles and sufferings is one of the greatest blessings and gifts in life. Suffering is easier to bear with support; this is true for everyone.

Who are the people whom we need to wrap a wall of love and care around? Obviously, those whom the Lord has placed in our lives are first to benefit from our care. Family and close acquaintances are the ones we must wrap a wall of love and care around continuously. All other people whom the Lord puts in our environment are also the ones whom we must care for and about in whatever way they need. We need to pay particular attention to other Christians in our world because we are all brothers and sisters in the family of Jesus, our head, and God our Father.

In Acts 4:32–37 and following, we read a description of how the early followers of Jesus changed their lifestyles, which changed the world, which was impressed and then convinced that this "new way" was beneficial for them, the pagans and many Jews alike. The love of Christians for each other is what made the early Christians survive the pagan world of the Roman Empire, and this love was what caused the Christian faith to spread throughout the known world. They built strong walls of love around each other to protect and take care of each one of them who were of the faith.

Our world greatly needs this kind of strong love to exist so that we can survive as Christians in our faith. There are virtues that we must possess so that we can build walls of love around other people. These include friendship, mutual respect, loyalty, gratitude, and sensitiveness toward others' feelings. Often, we must do battle with our own moods, passions, and temper to become loving, cheerful, and optimistic; some of us are not of that temperament. This is a suffering that we must not only endure but overcome; it is our duty. Those of us who have a critical, negative attitude, who speak harshly to and about others, who are easily annoyed, are those who are called "hypocritical" because this behavior is far from Christian teachings. This critical spirit is not of God, not of Jesus; it does not build loving walls, but walls of animosity.

It is not easy for this change to take place in us Christians; this is a major transformation, conversion. The conversion needed for us to be effective caregivers for other Christians must not be superficial; it requires time, effort, and a great grace from God, who will give us all we need as we ask for it.

Our work, our duty and responsibility, as Christians is to have God make changes in us as we struggle and pray so that we will be worthy protectors of others. Jesus gave us a new commandment: we are to love others as he loved us. In John 13:35, he says, "This is how all will know that you are My disciples, if you love one another."

1. What virtues do I need to focus on to become a better "brother"?
2. I will make new plans or revise those that I have made previously.
3. I will study some more Scripture passages.

Notes:

Chapter 8

Conversion Is Fearful

FROM OUR LESSONS, we have been learning that God created us for himself because he loved us, and he wants us to live in a close relationship with him. Jesus, his Son, was born with a human body. He lived and died among us to show us the Father's love, to teach us how to know, love, and serve God—the reason for our creation. He showed us that we must be obedient to God's will for us, which is the way that we will fulfill the purpose of our life. Why do we resist? Why do we employ some strategies to avoid complete conversion? We use these to partially follow Jesus. What are these?

Many of us are resistant because of the formula Jesus gave us to achieve God's purpose for our lives. He says that we must follow him, Jesus, and that this means we must pick up and carry our cross daily! Who wants that?

A great *fear* of suffering, caused by lack of knowledge of Scripture and Jesus's teachings, can keep us from total commitment (conversion). Many Christians, and others, believe that the suffering Jesus is talking about is as extreme as the cross and crucifixion of Jesus. Yes, there are extreme sufferings in the world. However, our daily crosses usually mean only the ordinary sufferings, difficulties, aggravations, failures, illnesses, heartbreaks, grief, rejections, loneliness that all mortals experience.

We learn that this means following God's will daily, faithfully, agreeably; we learn that when we do not accept God's will, or that we accept the suffering poorly, we *sin*. We learn that following Jesus means making reparation for our sins when we finally admit to sinning; finally, it means making a daily resolution to avoid sin. When we experience these "sufferings" as God's will for us, him allowing these difficulties, we can accept them as our daily crosses; this acceptance will bring peace, sometimes even joy, because we understand the need for suffering. When we resist these painful occurrences, we suffer more; and we can also cause others to suffer because of our negative attitudes and behaviors toward the problem we are going through. We can become angry, abusive, violent, depressed; this causes pain to those around us.

Also, we come to understand that "doing" this formula of Jesus is radical, that this calls for our almost total change of thinking and living! Saint Paul, in Ephesians 4:22, tells us that we must become a "new man." He tells us that we must throw off our "old self," which is us now! This is scary! This means that we must "work" hard and diligently to make the change. Many of us are afraid, many of us are too lazy, and many of us are not interested in the things of God. We refuse!

Another difficulty we often encounter in our desire for conversion is the *fright* of other consequences we may experience when we firmly accept Jesus's invitation. There is some basis for this fear. Faithful Christians are not friends of the world, who lives contrary to Christianity's values and morals; the world does not follow the commandments of God. This makes faithful Christians "out of step" with the world. The world does not tolerate this well; it causes us difficulties and problems in many ways.

To alleviate these fears and consequences, many of us do not make a total commitment, a total conversion to follow Jesus. Instead, we can choose a way of life that does not require the *courage* of totally turning our lives over to Jesus Christ, to our Christian faith. Many of us have fallen into the world's easier formula: God is love, they say, and so he cannot mean so strict a following of his laws. Many of us, therefore, have *softened* the commandments and the teachings of Jesus. We *do not use* words like *sin, reparation, atonement, punishment, hell.*

We can use Jesus's own words to avoid following Jesus closely. "I am meek and gentle of heart," Jesus says, so we rationalize that he will not be harsh with punishments. We ignore the words Jesus says in Matthew 7:21: "Not everyone who says Lord, Lord, will enter the kingdom, but only those who do the will of the Father." And we must remember Adam and Eve's disobedience; the punishment for us, their ancestors, continues even today.

Yes, God is love, *and* that means that he is a good parent. He disciplines his children (us) because he loves us, as do all good earthly parents. The Old Testament is a history of man's disobedience to God's commands and the devastating consequences that occurred. Therefore, God's will must be obeyed even through our hesitations and attempts to ease the fears and consequences of doing God's will in our earthly life.

Once we can admit our fear, laziness, and disinterest in the things of God, we are ready to make a firm decision to follow Jesus, who will lead us to God, to our home in heaven. This decision must include our acceptance of the purpose of our life: to know, love, and serve God and to be happy with him now and eternally. The mental struggle is over; however, the struggle to follow is not over until our last breath.

We must learn to face the fears we encounter daily as faithful Christians. And an important struggle is learning and defeating the subtle and not-so-subtle temptations from our own egos, the world, and the devil, all attempting to take us off our spiritual journey to God through our following of Jesus. He will, especially through the Holy Spirt, help us more and more as we progress. We are not alone. Amen.

1. Am I ready, or ready again, to start my conversion journey?
2. I will add this to the plans I have already made; I will add the study of spiritual books from holy people and support from other Christians.
3. I will study Scripture often; even fifteen minutes of study is helpful.

Notes:

Chapter 9

Practicing the Preaching

THERE IS GOOD news in today's culture of abusive language, anger, division, hatred, violence, and wars. There is a good answer to the bad news of this day. It is the same answer given over two thousand years ago. And we Christians can contribute to setting the world right now *in our own little world.* To do so, we will look at the problems we face; then we will focus on our part in the solutions.

The consequences of Adam and Eve's disobedience continue to this day. Their disobedience, their sin, causes us problems every day. They listened to the devil. They disobeyed the one rule that God had given them. They lost paradise. From that day on, they had suffering, a difficult life; and then they died, as we will all die too. None of this would have happened if they had not disobeyed. They lost paradise for themselves and for us, their descendants. We are born without the supernatural gifts that our first parents had before their sin. Their disobedience caused all of us an inherent weakness, like a genetic tendency to rebel. We tend to, and we do, disobey. This inherited stain is what is called the original sin. The result of this sin remains with all people always; the tendency to sin can cause us all untold troubles all our lives.

Today, we see the flagrant disobedience of the Ten Commandments, the bedrock of Christian society; these commandments have become irrelevant for most of Western societies. Christian values, morals, and way of life, as well as civil laws and rules, are regularly dismissed by many people, even baptized Christians. Many leaders in the media, government, business, even Christian churches have become the "wolves among the sheep" because many preach Christianity as the faith to live by, but many do not practice what they preach. Their hypocrisy weakens all of us; it causes many to flee from Christianity.

Many twenty-first-century people live outside of God's commandments and Jesus's teachings. In Philippians 3, Paul describes the life of the people of his time (and ours too). He tells us that their (and our) god is the belly: gluttony of food, drink, pleasures, lust. He warns us, like he warned them, about those who are leading an ungodly, shameful life, who even brag about it. (These are the people who accuse us Christians as being intolerant and judgmental because we cannot condone this behavior.)

We Christians who obey the commandments and Jesus's teachings, as well as the laws of our country and civil society, are often persecuted. We are ridiculed as being ignorant, uneducated, dumb, deplorable! Our children are taught by educators who undermine authority and religion's values and distort history to promote an agenda that is contrary to Christianity.

Where does this leave us who struggle to be faithful Christians? What is our responsibility, our duty, in this age of rampant disobedience? A call to arms! Our Christian faith is under attack; we must defend it! Your life, my life, can change the culture around us. Complaining, pointing fingers at others, angry arguments and words are not the answer.

We have work to do! *We* must change the culture around us by the kind of life that *we* live day by day. *We* must practice what *we* preach, *we* must live by the rules *we* say *we* believe in. Therefore, as Christians, we must follow what Jesus and his church teaches.

We must obey the laws of our country, our state, and our local government, unless the law is contrary to the laws of God. Do we break civil laws by using illicit drugs, by breaking speed limits? Do we cheat on our income taxes? And do we break the laws of God by gossiping, spreading scandals, speaking disrespectfully to and about other people, by overeating and drinking too much? Do we engage in sinful thinking, engage in watching sinful television and Internet sites? Engaging in these acts is dangerous because it can lead us to believe that they are not serious; this is a first step to more and more serious sins. Leaders in our world—in business, church, media, and politics—who do not follow the serious laws of God and man have more opportunities to commit serious sins. How would we deal with the temptations that they have? This is a subject we could meditate upon.

By our examples, sometimes by our words, we must quietly, peacefully, promote and teach the value and the benefits of obedience to all laws, all rules. We must work and pray for the conversion of all Christians who are not living the Christian life.

We must reform our own lives before we can expect others to change. God will show us how if we are open to hearing and following him. For example, when we say to ourselves, "I should not do this," but do it anyway, we are adding to the chaos in the world. When we say to ourselves, "I should do this," but do not do the good thing we have thought of, we may be missing God's inspiration and the opportunity to make some good thing in the world.

Lord, have mercy on us all as we do not always practice what we preach; we do not always do what we need to do, and we do what we should not do! Our world needs us to be better!

1. In what ways do I need to improve to make my world better?
2. I will review the plans I have made before; I will revise if needed.
3. I will continue to study Scripture often.

Notes:

Chapter 10

Deadly Pride

A CENTRAL COMMAND from God is that we must learn to know, love, and serve him; this is the reason why he created us, and he tells us that doing this will allow us to be happy with him now and eternally. A major character flaw many of us have that prevents us from even attempting to fulfill God's request is our *pride*, a great handicap that is so subtle that we can scarcely recognize it in ourselves. What is this deadly *pride*, this sin, and what is the opposite virtue that can save us? What are the dangerous results from *prideful* lives? How do we destroy in ourselves the kind of *pride* that harms us?

The *pride* that is deadly in the spiritual and physical world is the attitude that we do not need God; we believe ourselves to be independent of him. We certainly do not want to be submissive and obedient. This pride is what caused some angels to rebel against God; they said in effect, "We will not obey." God created them to serve; they said, "We will not serve." These are the devils who roam the world seeking to take us with them. And this same pride caused Adam and Eve to sin; they let Satan, the chief devil, trick them because they wanted to be "like gods," which was a lie. They too said, "We will not obey." (The world, under Satan's rule, tells us over and over that we do not have to obey. We are doing great on our own. We can control our own lives. God is too strict and demanding.)

Humility is defined as *truth*. Humility is the virtue that allows us to see that we are creatures whom God created out of nothing. On our own, we cannot take the next breath; we cannot add a minute to our life span. All the talents, gifts, opportunities that we call our own are given, allowed, provided for by God. *Pride* is the sin that denies that God has anything to do with our good gifts and situations, or we give God much less credit than we give to our own efforts. And the world continually backs this "I can do it on my own" mantra; God is not given any credit from this world.

Jesus taught that *pride* is a serious sin when he gives us the parable of the Pharisee and the tax collector (publican) praying in the temple, recorded for us in Luke 18:10. The Pharisee's prayer was unacceptable to God because his prayer was for himself, telling God how good he was, how much he was doing for God, and comparing himself to the "known" sinner, a tax collector. When we compare ourselves with others, saying how much better we are than they are, we are committing the sin of the proud person. The tax collector's prayer was accepted by God because he kept beating his breast, saying, "Have mercy on me, a sinner." He did not look up, kept his eyes downward in shame and guilt, not comparing himself with anyone. This man, the tax collector, made no excuses and only asked for mercy and forgiveness. His prayer is the pattern of a good confession.

Pride is the great enemy of spiritual growth and the enemy of a good relationship with God and others. When we are "full of ourselves," God cannot give us anything of himself, of his graces, of his own attributes. Then we are left with the weakness of our flawed human nature due to original sin. *Pride* destroys the soul's ability to let God's love make the soul like God himself. When we are "full of ourselves," others cannot give anything or much of themselves to us because there is no space available. When we believe that we are "good" as we are, when we believe that we do not need anything from God or others, we are listening to the world and the devil. We are in serious trouble!

How to we conquer *pride?* First, we continue learning to know Jesus and God through Jesus. We study the gospels and spiritual books and study groups to "see and hear" Jesus. This study will enable us to see how different our actions, our behaviors, and our thinking are from Jesus's. We will learn how far away we are from the virtue of *humility*, which is the great destroyer of *pride.*

An example from Scripture of the mercy and humility of God given to us from Jesus is recorded in Luke 15:20. Jesus tells the story of a young son who had left home and squandered his inheritance; and when he was starving, he recognized his inability to "do life" on his own. He returned home to his father. His father welcomed the prodigal son joyfully. The young son showed humility in return-ing to his father, admitting his sins and weaknesses. The eldest son, however, showed *pride* and a lack of mercy, angrily telling the father how good he had always been compared with his no-good younger brother.

We must do war against ourselves to "stamp out" misguided *pride.* (There is legitimate pride that is not unlawful or sinful or dan-gerous to our souls.) We must acquire humility, which requires great strength of character, great wisdom, and great courage. It requires God's help; it is too difficult to do alone because we are stained by original sin. *We resist obeying God; we do not want to submit.* We must admit that we are weak creatures totally dependent on God our Cre-ator, who gives us all the strength and power we need to obey.

Exchanging our sins of *pride* for the virtue of humility is what God wants for us, *not for himself.* He is perfectly happy; *he wants our happiness.* He created us to be happy, and he has the plan for our eternal happiness. We can choose to disregard God's blueprint; he has given us the freedom of choice. We can choose to reject him; the choice is ours. But let us remember that like the father in the parable of the prodigal son, God is always watching and waiting for us to come home to him. He loves us!

1. Am I aware of the sins of pride in myself? Do I have plans for growth of love for God and Jesus, including acquiring humility, shunning pride?
2. I will continue to study Jesus's life, searching for examples of his humility, his obedience to God.

Notes:

Chapter 11

Eternal Life Insurance

WE PURCHASE HEALTH, house, car, boat, life, liability, even burial insurance to protect ourselves and our loved ones from accidents, catastrophes that occur from forces of nature, from accidents, from illnesses, and from many other such occurrences. This is a wise response to the realities of our modern world. We do this; we feel safer. If we are truly wise, we know that our God is in charge, but it is smart that we do all we can. God expects this of us.

We Christians know that this life on earth is a journey to our God and to our everlasting life. Surely, the most important insurance, therefore, is for that eternal life. The Holy Scripture reminds us that our earth life is short. For example, Psalm 90:10 tells us that a man's life is seventy years, eighty if he is strong. (And these verses also tell us that most of these years are spent with troubles and sorrow!) Many of us are called sooner, sometimes much sooner. It is now uncommon that young people, even children, die. Now we are in the midst of a pandemic, and hundreds of thousands have died, and many more will succumb to this disease and many other dreaded diseases. Surely, we need to examine our lives in terms of insurance for eternity.

How do we purchase this most important of all insurances? We do not purchase this insurance with money, but with our actions, with the kind of life we lead. We must spend our lives doing what God has created us to do: knowing, loving, serving him, mostly by serving others, like our families and our communities. To make sure that we pay the correct amount of the premiums of this insurance correctly, we follow Jesus's teachings, God's commandments. This is the cost of heaven, the physical and mental costs of this guarantee to eternal life's rewards or punishments.

With our death, Jesus, the just judge, can no longer extend his blessings, his loving mercy, his graces, his sacraments, which he has left for us in his church for our journey back to him, to God. God has made us for the particular purpose of knowing, loving, serving others in this time, place, situation where he has placed us. But the time is up with our death. We have had days, months, years, even many decades. Important now is what we have done with this time. What gifts have we used for our eternal life? What gifts have we ignored, neglected, misused? What is the accumulated capital that we will take with us when we breathe our last breath?

No one knows for sure how our whole life's actions will be revealed, but we do know that what will be revealed will result in eternal damnation or eternal happiness in heaven, perhaps with some time for purification first. We recall that Jesus's last words on the cross were, "It is finished." Then he breathe his last; he commended his soul to God. These words refer to the fact that the purpose of his life, the command of his Father, is done. His work here on earth is finished. After our last breath, we too will say or hear, "It is finished." The assignment we have been given to do is turned in—well done, poorly done, ignored!

What will be the standard, the tests, by which we will be judged? Jesus came to show us how to fulfill the plan that God has for our lives. He came to teach us, to give himself totally to us, even to die for us. Now he will judge us as to the "fruits of his labors;" the standard will be his life and his teachings.

We know with certainty that we must know and love God, our Creator and Father, Jesus, our Savior and teacher, the Holy Spirit, dispenser of God's graces. We must love and serve our family, neighbors, friends, and many others who are in our lives. While there is still time, we can learn and practice how to love. Even though we are old, young, healthy, sick, bored, busy, rich, or poor, there is *today* in which we can love. It is never too late. While there is breath, there is time to love, to increase the value of our whole life insurance.

1. If I know that I do not know how to love and serve well, am I willing to start learning? Will I add this to my plan for spiritual growth?

2. Who in my life do I need to love more? What specific actions will I take?

3. I will continue to study Scripture to learn how to love and serve.

Notes:

Chapter 12

The Fire of Love

FIRE IS IMPORTANT for us; it fuels many aspects of our lives. Much of what is super important to our world would disappear without the heat, the fuel of fire. Love is like a fire; love fuels and heats one's zeal for service, for sharing, for working to fulfill goals, and especially for creating and maintaining relationships. How does this fire of love begin and develop? How does it grow, and what can diminish or destroy the fire of love? What are the benefits for us?

Passion, the feeling that can accompany love, is the desire to do and to want what is best for the other (others) involved. Love is not a feeling; real love (*agape*) is the actions done for the good of the other. Romantic, sexual attraction and feelings are often mistaken for *agape, which is love with or without much feelings.* There is much misunderstanding of this in our culture. Love is the doing of good; it is not a feeling.

Intimate contact with God produces fiery love, which moves the soul to have zeal for his service. On fire with love, we want and need to share this love; we want to tell all how good, generous, loving God is. We want to serve by serving those around us and those in our communities, our whole world. An example of this kind of love can be the father who loves his wife and children so much that he loves, helps, supports all those whom his family loves. This is the kind of love that God has for us. Fire can be a misused passion, like a wildfire in a forest, which consumes everything in its path, leaving destruction, pain, sorrow. God's love, Jesus's love, is not this kind of love; it is the wildfire that destroys sin, faults, imperfections, selfishness in our souls. What is left is joy, peace, vibrant energy all around us.

The fire of love for the Lord begins like the fire of love for anyone on the human level. First, we are attracted to the person. Then we proceed to get to know about him. Then we spend time with that person to grow closer. This is the time that little children want to know about God, Jesus, heaven; it is an important time to carefully introduce them especially to the goodness and love of Jesus for them. But too often, we parents, and other important people in the lives of our children, do not continue to foster and fuel this awakening interest (fire of love); their interest stops. The children grow into adolescence and adulthood without the knowledge and love for Jesus growing in step with their physical and mental growth; their spiritual growth is stunted. (Many of us adults are at this place in our spiritual life.)

At some point, and perhaps many times, in our adult life, we have had an opportunity to let an "attraction" to God, to Jesus, to church, grow. The interest may have been sparked during a Christian wedding or funeral, a homily by a Christian pastor or layperson, a movie or book. The interest disappears, wanes, because we do nothing to increase it. It just becomes comatose. It may not be dead, but it is not responding to life. On the other hand, sadly, many of us never had an interest in the things of God.

One reason that our fire of love for God, for Jesus, dies is the same reason why the love of spouses, family members, friends can die. Lack of the investment of time with each other leads to lack of knowledge and understanding of what the other person is doing, feeling, coping in their lives. The less we know, the more disinterest grows. Finally, the love dies. This never happens on God's part; he is always with us and is interested in us because he loves us no matter whether we love him or not. (For one reason or another, some of us never have had an interest in God.) This disinterest in the other—spouse, family, friend—most often happens gradually. Often, the damage of the disinterest can be recognized in time and be mended. Sometimes the love dies permanently. Love can die or never begin because we are totally concerned with things of the world; this can be because the many pleasures available to us in our modern world consume us. The investments of our time in hobbies, work, careers, politics, or business enterprises can take too much of our days and energy, which leaves none for important relationships, like that with God and others.

Another characteristic that we can acquire that can contribute to smothering the fire of love or never allowing it to grow is being lukewarm. This condition, which we have been specifically warned about and which is recorded in Revelations 3:16, tells us that "because we are neither hot nor cold [lukewarm] toward God, he will vomit us out of His mouth." This is a very graphic picture. Lukewarm is selfishness, laziness, neglectfulness of our responsibilities to give to others what should be theirs because of the responsibilities that we owe to them, like neglecting aging parents or a spouse or children or siblings.

So how do we fan the flames of love for God? The first three commandments that God gave us are about our duties to God himself; he demands our reverence and our time. We are not to put anything or anyone before God; for example, nothing is more important than reverencing him on Sundays, his holy day.

The importance of prayer cannot be overemphasized; formal prayers and spontaneous prayer, the lifting of our hearts and minds up to God often every day, will make the flames of love burn brighter. Meanwhile, practicing charity (love) constantly for all those in our lives by faithfully performing the duties of our state of life, our vocations, and doing these primarily for God, keeps the love friendships with God and others alive and healthy.

We Christians who love God and Jesus experience great joy and peace, which are God's gifts to us; these are not the temporary joy and peace the world offers. Then we share the joy, peace, and love of God with others who are around us; the fire of love spreads. God gives the love, joy, and peace; we pass them on. God takes our small works of love and increases these a hundredfold until there is a burning furnace of love in the whole world.

1. What plans have I made to intensify my love for God? For others?

2. What am I doing to "pass the fire of love" to others?

Notes:

Chapter 13

Avoiding Great Tragedy

A REAL TRAGIC situation for many of us is that Jesus is unimportant in our lives; many of us do not see, know, or recognize Jesus in our daily lives. Many of us have been able to see Jesus from time to time, but not often; perhaps we had known Jesus in our daily activities and in the stillness of our hearts, but we seem to have lost him. Perhaps we have never known, felt, or experienced Jesus in our lives. Some of us go through our days as if Jesus does not exist, as if his death and resurrection did not happen. Some of us think that Jesus's death and resurrection did happen, but we do not believe that it matters in our lives in the here and now.

Thanks be to God, many of us do decide that we need and want to focus on our spiritual, eternal life; we want to know, love, and serve God. What to do if we want to change our attitude (and our lives), although we do not "feel" anything, but we "know" we strongly believe that it is necessary to do this now? There are steps that we can take to avoid the greatest tragedy in one's life: no closeness to Jesus, who is "the way, the life, the truth" of life.

When we really want to know, see, and experience Jesus in our lives every day, what do we do? Or if we knew him, how and why did we lose him? How can we avoid losing him again? The *desire* for this conversion is the necessary first step; Jesus, like the father in the parable of the prodigal son, has been looking and waiting for us. His love, mercy, and concern are immediately put into action with our desire.

The most obvious step after desiring to convert our lives to get close to Jesus, to God, is to ask for their help. *Prayer* is the way to get God's immediate attention, along with the desire to convert. Many times, in many ways, Jesus, the one who is God, has told us how to get close to him and the Father and the Holy Spirit. The Our Father prayer is one sure way to do this. Also, Jesus tells us, as recorded in Matthew 7:7–8, "Ask and it will be given you; knock and the door will be opened to you. For everyone who asks receives; and the one who seeks, finds; and to the one who knocks, the door will be opened to him." Jesus is always waiting at the door of our hearts to open his heart to us! We must talk to him; that talking is prayer. We speak in formal prayers, in spontaneous talks, telling him of our needs, our thanks; we do this silently or aloud! Jesus hears our voices, our minds, and our hearts.

As we all know, in our natural, physical life, when we want to get to know a subject or a person, we must devote *time* to this endeavor. When we want to get to know Jesus, we must spend much time with him. We give him specific times in prayer; this is very necessary. We learn to "talk" to him always. We ask for his help when we are suffering and in pain, when we are grieving and cannot understand why this is happening to us. We ask for his support to help solve problems, make decisions. We ask him to help us overcome bad habits and sins. We ask for forgiveness for what we have done and what we have failed to do every day. *And it is important to thank him for all that happens, for all the graces he sends us. Gratitude* is a very loving way to get close to anyone, including God and Jesus.

Another important step to remain close to Jesus is to understand and live by the knowledge that *we are made in the likeness of God [our souls, not our bodies]; God is all-holy; we must become like Him: holy.* We must align our lives with Jesus's life. The original sin we inherited from Adam makes it difficult for us to become holy, to follow Jesus closely. We must give up our sins; we must follow the commandments of God and all the teachings of Jesus; doing this will put us on the correct road to close relationships with them. But because we love some of our sins, it is difficult for us to give them up. The habits we have acquired, sinful habits or not, are hard to change;

other habits do not come easily. Also, some of our sins may involve other people, which makes matters more complicated. God is merciful and all-knowing; he knows our situations. When we desire to make necessary changes and ask him for help, he will.

The solution to the problems of our sins will be done in God's time; we must be patient and continue to pray. We must continue to follow Jesus's teachings as well as we can in these conditions.

God loves us more than we love ourselves. He sent Jesus to show us this great love, to teach us how to know and return God's love. Jesus died for us in order to give us the true picture of God's love. He rose from the dead to prove to us that he is God. He instituted a church, guided by the Holy Spirt, whom he sent when he ascended into heaven. He gave us all we need to know, love, and serve God and be eternally happy with him. Therefore, we can avoid the great tragedy of no relationship with Jesus, with God; the choice is ours to do what is necessary! The plan is simple to understand, but it will take our entire lives to achieve it.

1. Do my plans for conversion allow much prayer time? Have I started working on the habit of talking to Jesus, to God the Father, all day long? Will I?
2. I will meditate on Scripture readings to continue to know, love, and serve God.

Notes:

Chapter 14

Great Duty of Service

WE READ IN Mark 9:33–37 that the disciples of Jesus were arguing about which of them was the greatest, the most important in the group around Jesus. Jesus gave them a brutal, vivid answer to their debate, probably dashing their hopes for royal leadership. He told them, as recorded in Matthew 21:26–27, that the greatest among them must be the servant of all. Then, to further dismay these unsuspecting disciples, Jesus told them that he himself, the living God, came to serve and save mankind, not to be served. He also told them that he was to be the ransom for all; they certainly did not understand that they were captives who needed ransoming—from whom?

It was too early in Jesus's life for the disciples to understand how Jesus served them, served us. But we have all the facts: Jesus was killed to ransom us from the chains of sin by which Satan had bound mankind when Adam and Eve had disobeyed. Paradise was closed to us sinners; only a divine person could reopen it. So Jesus was killed, rose from the dead, reopened paradise, established his religion, Christianity. He did all that "service" to show his love for us.

Jesus tells us Christians that we are to be unlike the rest of the world; we are not to fight to be in authority. Our command is that we must all serve each other, and that the greatest among us, the one with legitimate authority, must be the servant of all! Instead, by his example, Jesus showed us that God, the Creator of all that is, came to serve. This is Jesus's way of telling us that those of us who have more (talents, skills, money, etc.), more is required from us.

A great danger for us is the message we hear so often. The world does not advocate serving others as a worthy goal. Our modern world teaches us to promote ourselves, make ourselves evident, in the limelight if possible. We are groomed to "shine"; we are pushed to compete. And certainly, we are not taught to accept being "last" and be someone who serves others.

How do we acquire this state of mind, this Christian way? How do we reject the world and the devil's message? Christianity, Jesus's religion, teaches that the great virtue of humility is the answer to fulfilling Jesus's teaching, his commandment to love by serving. *Humility is defined as truth. Truth* makes us know ourselves as we truly are. *Truth* demands that we take our proper place, the place where we belong, because God has placed us here. This means that *we must serve where we are placed.* The more modern quote "Bloom where you are planted" is perfect. The quote explains that in this place, in these circumstances, with what we have in talent, intelligence, opportunity, we are to "bloom"; and Jesus says "serve" in that spot! This is the place where Jesus needs us to help him take care of others.

The virtue of humility prevents us from lying, cheating, fighting to achieve "the spot" we desire. Those of us with "more" are to accept our higher position, in which God has placed us, with the knowledge that we are to *serve more, not less, than others.* Those of us who have "less" in some way or another are not to attempt to be *who we are not!* This leads to a "false self," not the self that God created.

Back to the basic *truth* that Jesus gave us: we are all to *serve.* The more we have, the more responsible we are to give, to help, to support. We are all equal in God's eyes; we are all his creatures. We are all totally dependent on him for our life, our next breath. None of us can perform any action on our own. The richest man on the planet, the poorest one, the most intelligent man, the most mentally disabled, the most educated person, the most uneducated, *all—all totally depend on our Lord and our God.* As Paul asks us, in 1 Corinthians 4:7, why do we claim glory in what we have, what we have done? God gave us all of this?

The Christian path is to be guided by Jesus's commandments, in humility, to love others by serving them. When we esteem ourselves, honestly and fairly, as God created us, when we follow his plan for our lives, then we will serve in peace and serenity. We cannot improve on God's plans.

1. Am I "serving" with the best effort, talent, time that I have? If not, why?
2. In his plan for our life, we will find our true place. Then we will serve in that place in peace. And how else can I serve? Whom else can I serve?

Notes:

Chapter 15

Jesus, True God and True Man

IN THE SEVENTEENTH century, the Jansenism heresy arose, confused many people, and led them into dark and evil places. Basically, Jansenism teaches that we must be "perfect" before we can approach God, that we are too sinful, too unworthy of God's admitting us into his presence. Artists painted God as an angry, fierce-looking, ugly man looking to cast us into hell.

What does that have to do with us in the twenty-first century? What is the great truth that refutes, destroys this heresy?

Jansenism is relevant today because it advocates that this angry, vengeful God does not want us to have joy, fun; he wants us to be sad, never happy. To the followers of Jansenism, God is always looking to punish us! Now, that is what the world teaches about Christianity. That is one reason why the world distorts Christianity in order to make it appear as a negative, judgmental, oppressive religion. This attitude toward God and Christianity was evil in the beginning of Jansenism; it is an evil tool of the devil today. Sadly, it is preached loudly and clearly in the mass media channels of this century! Sadly, it is still leading many souls astray, even some baptized Christians, who are poorly educated in Christianity's teachings.

We Christians know (should know) that this teaching is the opposite of what and who God is because Jesus, who is God, the Second Person of the Trinity, lived as a Man among us for thirty-three years; he showed us, by his life, the nature of God, which is totally opposite of Jansenism's false teachings. The Gospels tell us some of what Jesus did and taught. All records of Jesus's life give the message that he came to bring us: God loves us tremendously, and God is loving, merciful, always caring for us, his children. Because of his divine nature, Jesus could not reveal totally the extent of God's love because we are not capable of understanding this mystery. However, we learn as much as we want to know about the nature of God from the life, words, and actions of Jesus in Scripture.

John 11:33–36 tells us that Jesus is perfect God and perfect Man. We know that Jesus showed human love and friendship. When his friend Lazarus died, Jesus was grieved by the death, and by Lazarus's sister Mary's great sorrow shown by much shedding of tears. Although he knew that he was going to perform the great miracle of raising Lazarus from the dead, Jesus was still so saddened by all this human sorrow that he (God) *wept*; we read this account in John 11:5.

Near the end of his time here on earth, Jesus traveled to Jerusalem, where he had preached and performed many miracles; Jesus loved this city. But the hard-hearted Jewish leaders and their followers rejected him; they would soon put him to death, as he well knew. As he approached the city, Jesus became sad and sorrowful because, as recorded in Luke 19:14–44, Jesus knew that this city that he loved so much would be destroyed because of their rejection of him. In his sorrow over the coming destruction of this holy place, *Jesus wept.*

When we explore the Gospels, we see Jesus tired, hungry, concerned for the needs of others, performing miracles to help cater to physical, mental, and spiritual needs, including providing wine at the happy wedding feast at Cana. We read his beautiful, simple-to-understand teachings in the Gospels. Jesus, our loving friend, is still alive today! He is still seeking our love and friendship; he is still being rejected, even by Christians. Let us not saddened him; let us reject and deny the lies taught by the teachers of Jansenism and other heresies.

1. I will study gospel passages that show Jesus's humanity.
2. As I read about what Jesus was doing, I will meditate on what he might have been feeling as a human man, while he healed and taught the people in the gospels.

Notes:

Chapter 16

Jesus in Heaven

WE CHRISTIANS ARE faced with many mysteries that call for trust in God. Some mysteries are revealed in Scripture; some are not. There are many beliefs that may be "fuzzy" in our minds, but we obey Jesus's teachings and our church's teachings that we do not fully understand and cannot fully reason. We will not know everything until the Final Judgment at Jesus's Second Coming—or before at our personal judgement. (That too is a mystery.)

One mystery that Christians have studied and meditated upon is the suffering-God mystery, Jesus, true God and true Man, in heaven. Let us explore, study, understand Jesus's sufferings on earth as well as in heaven.

One thing we do know, in order to know, love, serve God, the purpose of our lives, we must follow the commandments and laws of God as revealed in the Scriptures, as well as the traditions, preserved in the church and handed down through the generations. We are commanded by God, as our Creator, and taught by Jesus that we are to obey; disobedience causes what we know as *sin*.

One reason *not* to sin is that it *harms us!* Sin deforms our character; it deforms that part of us that has been made in the "image of God" as told in Genesis 1:27. If we are not "like him," we may not be able to be with him in heaven, our destination, our home. Jesus, the God-Man does not want this to happen to us; he wants us with him and the Father. When we refuse, he is saddened, as are the other two persons of the Blessed Trinity.

Another reason why we do not want to sin is that it *harms others*, sometimes severely. All the commandments command us not to harm others. When we harm others, the Blessed Trinity is saddened for us and for the one whom we harmed.

It is also our Christian belief that our sins offend, hurt, even anger *God*. God is spirit, and he is love. He responds to our lives on earth because he cares so much for us; like all parents, God finds disobedience hurtful. However, with God, the hurt is not to him alone; the hurt is to us too. *Sin hurts us,* and God, who loves us so much, does not want us to sin because he sees sin hurting us; we are his beloved! Imagine!

After Adam and Eve's disobedience, man's history has been a history of paganism, brutality, violence of man upon man. God intervened at a certain time in man's history; God appointed Abraham to separate himself from his peers and relatives and to start a new family, a new nation in a new territory: the Jewish nation. The Old Testament is the history of this nation, which time after time disobeyed, was "corrected" by God, rose and fell, rose and fell, until that nation finally believed in the one true God. They were promised a Messiah; they believed, wrongly, that the Messiah was going to be a great worldly king who would free them from their Roman captives.

Over two thousand years ago was the time that God chose to send Jesus, the Second Person, the Son, the Messiah. It appeared that at least some of the people were ready to receive the Messiah, the one who opened the door to heaven, which had been closed by Adam's sin. He is Savior and Redeemer. (He was rejected by most of the Jewish nation because Jesus was not like the king they had expected the Messiah to be.)

But Jesus came also to show us, to emphasize, not only the God who disciplines but also the parental side of God, our Father. God disciplines by allowing the consequences of disobedience; but God is, most of all, the tender, loving, merciful God who loves each of us more than we can comprehend. In fact, God is *love*. Jesus on the cross is the measure of God's love for us! We know that Jesus, both God and Man, wept over Lazarus' death and his sister's suffering; Jesus wept over the impending destruction of Jerusalem because it would not accept him as sent by God the Father as Messiah and Son of God.

Now that Jesus is in heaven, a place of eternal happiness, does he still weep over our rejection of him, our refusal to follow him? One explanation given for our understanding of the suffering God is that Jesus is the head of the body, his church here on earth. We believe that we are all members of that one body, and that any sin, pain, suffering that we experience or cause, causes pain to Jesus's body, the church. Saint Paul in 1 Corinthian 12:12–26 explains this very well for us. Jesus himself tells us, as recorded in Saint Matthew 20:25, that anything that we do to any of the least of his people, we do to him.

But the head of the body, Jesus, is in heaven; how can he be affected by what we do here on earth? Some theologians, other holy people, mystics, tell us that in some mysterious way, Jesus suffers (is affected somehow); while in heaven in his divinity, he, Jesus, is also Man. Those who advocate this belief cite Saul's episode in Act 9:4, when Jesus asked Saul, renamed Paul, "Why are you persecuting *me*?" Jesus did not ask Paul, "Why are you hunting my disciples, imprisoning them?" He specified that Paul was hunting *him, Jesus.*

What a mystery that is! On this side of heaven, the mystery can only be speculated about. One recent pope observed that it is humanly possible to believe that a mother could be very happy *and* saddened at the same time by the suffering of one of her children. We do not know; we do not have to know.

What is important for us in our pilgrimage to God is to realize that we have the "plan" from a loving God; he has given us the tools: Jesus, the Holy Scripture, the church, the Holy Spirit. The mysteries that we do not need to understand now are God's business; trusting him is our business.

1. Which of God's characteristics do I associate most with: his love and mercy, his ability to help me, his disciplines and punishments? Some other characteristic?
2. What do I need to do to develop more faith and trust in his love for me? Make a list.

Notes:

Chapter 17

Religion of Love

A COMMON COMPLAINT about Christians is that we are too negative. Critics say, "Christianity is all about 'Do not...'" Critics complain that Christians are negative, judgmental, hypocritical. Many of us are guilty of this; many of us sometimes are. But many Christians are accused of being judgmental because *we refuse to accept what is sinful, evil, immoral as being good.*

Let us explore the background of God's dealing with his people and the development of Jesus's religion from the Old Testament and how loving this religion, as shown in the Old Testament, has been. Jesus's religion, Christianity, as shown in the New Testament, is truly a religion of love.

Let us explore the background of the foundation of Christianity in the Old Testament. God provided rules and laws, through Moses, like the Ten Commandments, to teach a nation that had lived in the pagan land of Egypt and that was ignorant of the one God. They were to learn that they were created by a God whose name is "I am who am"; this is recorded for us in Exodus 3:14. Moses taught the Israelites that they were to obey this God, who would make them his own people, who would protect and cherish them. The Jewish nation was taught obedience through the great punishments inflicted upon them when they disobeyed; they were not ready for the God who is love. This obeying and disobeying, falling and rising, continued for thousands of years until God saw that this nation could obey and understand. Then he sent his Son, Jesus, to live among them to teach them and us and all generations who will come after us.

The language of Jesus's religion helped us to "see" the commandments of God from the Old Testament in a different way, but he did not change or abolish God's commandments and rules.

Jesus came to fulfill the promises given in the Old Testament; his words are recorded for us in Matthew 5:17–19.

Some examples will make clearer Jesus's approach to the commandments. Jesus says, "Blessed are the poor in spirit, for theirs is the kingdom of heaven." Jesus is asking that we work but not anxiously, feverishly, to gain material goods and power. He tells us to depend on God's help and to be content with God's providence for us. This embraces the commandments of "Thy shall not steal" and "Thy shall not covet [greatly desire] your neighbor's goods." To be poor in spirit enables us to look to the God, who loves us and provides for us as we do our work. And we see our neighbor as one whom God loves also; therefore, we do not envy his good fortune.

Jesus says, "Blessed are the clean of Heart, for they will see God." Our hearts, thoughts, memory, imagination must be pure, avoiding temptations and lustful desires. The commandments "Thy shall not commit adultery" and "Thy shall not covet your neighbor's wife" and other sins of the flesh will not be broken if we are "clean and pure" in our thinking, running away from temptation, and praying much. Today's culture promotes immorality and persecutes those of us who protest. It can be difficult to retain purity; God must assist us.

Jesus says, "Blessed are the meek, for they will inherit the earth." He is advocating being gentle, patient, understanding, *but courageous with great strength of character.* This requires the ability to control strong emotions, passions, like anger, hatred, jealousy. This prevents breaking the commandment of "Thy shall not kill." Jesus's new law is *"Love your neighbor as yourself."*

The early Christian changed the culture of the mighty Roman Empire. We can also change our own anti-Christian culture! We *can learn the beautiful, positive teachings of Jesus. We can live these positive teachings.* When all who profess being Christian follow Jesus, who is the way, the truth, and the life, others may come to believe and be converted as the Romans were; we read this in John 14:6. Christianity is gentle but strong, courageous, determined in the spiritual battle that rages in the twenty-first century. Jesus has told us many times, "Be not afraid." Saint Paul in Philippians 4:13 encourages us when he tells that we can do everything through him who strengthens us. The early Christians experienced terrible persecutions, and many of them died joyfully. The furious battles against Christianity continue; history has shown that Christianity has always been persecuted. The world ruled by the devil will always battle fiercely against Jesus's religion; we read about this in John 8:42.

Let us again follow Jesus in the "religion" of the early church. Jesus taught, by his words and actions and emotions, the deeper, more positive spirit of God's commandments, which were given in the Old Testament. We follow the commandments because Jesus taught us these are rules for our own good, our benefit, because of God the Father's love for us. The Old Testament's history did not emphasize God's love because the people were not ready for this; they needed to fear God first. Hopefully, we follow the commandments out of love, although fear is sometimes necessary to encourage obedience; ask parents!

1. I will list and study the Beatitudes. (Luke 6: 20-26)
2. I will list and study the Sermon on the Mount. (Matthew 5:1-12)

Notes:

Chapter 18

Lessons Learned from an Old Man

THERE ARE MULTITUDES of lessons that are relevant for us to learn from the Bible; we will look at one episode that can help us who are seeking to know, love, and serve God.

In Luke 2:25–32, we read the episode of the holy man Simeon, who was "righteous and devout," to whom the Holy Spirit had revealed that he would not die until he had seen the Messiah of the Lord. Simeon, like all devout Jews at this time, was waiting for a Messiah who would restore God's authority in Israel, which was now under the pagan Roman Empire's rule. Simeon came into the temple when Mary and Joseph brought Jesus in "to perform the custom of the law," the presentation of the firstborn male in a family. Simeon recognized Jesus as Messiah. Simeon took Jesus into his arms; he blessed God for allowing him to see the Messiah. Simeon predicted Jesus would be contradicted, and that both Jesus and Mary would suffer much. But Simeon's faith in God's promise was rewarded; he knew that this child was his Savior. How did Simeon know? Did he have special powers? We will study further.

What about us? Do we recognize Jesus as the Messiah in our daily life? Is the story of Simeon something that happened over two thousand years ago and is not relevant to us today? Not so! The Holy Scripture's messages are timeless; whatever is revealed is for all generations, until time ends (Hebrew 13:8). God's messages are for us as they were for Simeon and his peers. But it seems that only Simeon recognized Jesus as the Messiah. Perhaps, he was the only one interested.

What about us? Do we believe that we need a Savior? Do we believe we need to be saved? We must believe or we will not seek him. Let us review the reason why we need to be saved. Adam and Eve were cast out of the Garden of Eden, heaven, when they listened to the devil and disobeyed God. They could not return to heaven, and they were now slaves of Satan. As their children, we too are born as slaves to Satan and cannot get to heaven; that is the reason why we need a Savior. Our merciful God promised a Messiah, a Savior, who would break the devil's hold over the descendants of Adam, us, and reopen the gates to heaven. This Savior was Jesus—is Jesus!

To recognize our Savior, Jesus, today as Simeon did centuries ago, we must be "looking" as he was. We must believe, and we must be watching, observing, and expecting God's promise that we can live in God's kingdom, freed from Satan's hold on us if we choose. We were promised this in the Old Testament; Jesus brought this to us. The New Testament is a record of this promise and its fulfillment, telling us that we are now children of God.

We must admit that our world is mostly pagan; the one true God and the religion that Jesus established over two thousand years ago have become irrelevant for many people. We must be like Simeon, who "kept the faith." We must be looking for God's acting in our lives. We must be like Simeon, waiting patiently and "on guard," to recognize him in our daily lives. It may be difficult for us to be aware that Jesus is here; he has brought God's kingdom to us now on this earth. We must be vigilant in seeking to recognize him and the kingdom.

We do not have to wait as Simeon did to find the Messiah. We can find the Messiah in the book of Jesus's life and of the early church: the New Testament. We can study this book of Jesus's life and teachings, especially the Gospels; and we can learn for ourselves how Jesus was living, what he was doing, what he was saying. We can learn what God is like, his laws, his goodness, and his mercy, by studying Jesus in the Gospels. And we can live in the kingdom by following his teachings, by being in and of his church, by fighting the world and the devil's tactics.

Only our indifference, our laziness, our immersion in this world can keep us from knowing and recognizing Jesus as the Savior we need constantly in our lives to defend us from the evil around us and from the evil we are capable of doing. If we want to know and love Jesus in our daily lives, there is a multitude of spiritual books to study, spiritual and prayer groups to join, media sources to search; our faithful church pastors and other faithful Christians are available to help us. We only have to "seek and we will find" Jesus and the kingdom, heaven on earth, the beginning of our eternal life.

Yes, Simeon has something to teach us; look for the Lord! We can find him in his words and his life in the Holy Bible; we can find him in prayer, in our family and loved ones whom he gave us, and in the events in our world! Unlike Simeon, we do not have to wait for years, for decades, to see Jesus. The Lord is here; he is not hidden. He is close to us always.

1. Where did I find Jesus today? Event? Person? Was I looking when I recognized him?
2. Did I thank Jesus for allowing me to recognize him and his works in my life?

Notes:

Chapter 19

Going Nowhere

THE ISRAELITES WANDERED in the desert for forty years, not reaching the Promised Land because they continuously disobeyed God, who spoke directly to them through Moses. We think, *How crazy was that?* Yet too many of us Christians who have been ransomed, taught, sanctified by Jesus and his church continue walking in the "desert," going nowhere, disoriented in this passing world; we have given little or no thought to our "eternal destination after this short life." In fact, many of us do not know or care what God has ordained as the purpose of our lives.

If we have this frame of mind, this attitude, what effect does this have on our lives, our eternal life, the life of others? What are we expected to do?

Without a strong purpose for our lives, we can go "nowhere"; that is, we can go far from the place we need to be. We were created to know, love, and serve God and others on earth, and then be happy forever in our real home, heaven. How many of us think that we are here on earth "to pass a good time," make money, take material care of our family, help others if it is not too much trouble? Too many of us seem to think that some big problems are for others to solve; we may just analyze, "talk about" problems, but we do little or nothing to solve social problems, problems in our environment, our nation, our church. But God thinks differently; that is not why he created us. None of us can be exempted from actively doing something to better the lives of others and the conditions of the community in which we live; none of us can be exempted, without eternal consequences, from learning to know, love, serve God and others. Whether we know it or not, whether we like it or not, all of us are expected to fulfill God's purpose for creating us, to serve God by serving others in our world.

For example, what can we do about the many problems in our own little world? In the chaos around us? Have we helped or worsened the serious problems around us? Have we prayed more? Have we joined prayer groups? Have we helped clean our environment? Have we written letters to elected officials? Have we donated money to worthy causes? Kept in touch with friends, relationships, who are ill or weak or disabled? Have we offered the talents we have to our church, our city? We need not search for what needs to be done; everyday, we see "need" all around, *if we look.*

Many of us Christians will arrive at the end of life asking ourselves what "good" we accomplished in our life. We may come to life's end knowing all the goals we have achieved—work, money, power, pleasures—have faded away; much of life will flash by, empty now. Far too many of us will realize that the people and the events in our lives have not caused us to be better followers of Christ. Nor have we made others better Christians. We may realize that we are "okay," "good" people, but that's it. God's plan for our lives, to grow in deep knowledge, love, and service of the God and others, has not been "our plan." We may have gone through decades of "not bad but not really good" disciples of Jesus Christ. Will that matter? Jesus has told us that because we are lukewarm toward him, "he will vomit us out of his mouth," that is, "reject" us! This passage, found in Revelations 3:16, is *scary!*

Matthew 7:22–23 tells us that Jesus told us that he would judge us by the fruit of our lives, which must be living and doing what God has created us to be and do; otherwise, when we knock on his door for entrance, he may tell us, "I never knew you." We may tell Jesus that we went to church, we were baptized, confirmed, and followed most of the commandments and Jesus's teachings most of the time. Evidently, that is not enough, for he will say, "Go away. I do not know you." We may well find out that it is *"not only what we have done wrong or badly, but what good have we not done, what good have we neglected to do."* That teaching is not often emphasized; most of us do not really meditate on the need "to do." While there is time for us, we must no longer neglect. Let us start today.

1. Today I will review and examine myself in terms of becoming more aware of the purpose for which God created me.
2. I will make a serious decision to focus my life on God's purpose for me or recommit myself.
3. I will study the Scripture reading listed.

Notes:

Chapter 20

God Institutes Love:
Jesus Teaches It

THE QUOTE "LOVE is repaid by love alone" is attributed to Saint Thérèse of Lisieux. Almost all of us understand the meaning and truth of this quote. Only by deeds do we show our love for another person. And all our thoughts, words, actions, in terms of the other person, are for their best interests; we want "only the best" for the ones we love.

God' love is unique; he commands us to love him and others as he does. Jesus is the one who came to show and teach us about God's great love and the way we are to love.

God created us to *love him.* He has no need of us; he wanted to share his glory and his goodness. He created us in "his image and likeness," we are told in the book of Genesis. God created us just as he wanted us, at the time and place he wanted. Psalm 139 recounts the story of our being formed, knitted by God in our mothers' wombs, in secret, by all, even our own mothers; only he who was "knitting" us as he wanted knew our secret body and soul! Awesome!

God loves us! That is an awesome reality; if we can wrap our heads around this, if we can come to really believe this, our life might be changed forever! Achieving this awareness, most of us find that this reality is a process. We only come to believe this, to internalize this truth, slowly; sadly, some of us never do *learn* this glorious truth.

God's love for us is eternal; he has always had us in his mind and his heart! At some point in time when he was ready for us, he created us and did so just like he wanted us to be. And now he "hovers" over each one of us as though we are the "only child" he has. No matter our age, *each one of us is his child.* God's love is unconditional; it does not depend on who we are, what we have done, what we are doing, what we will do. God loves us individually forever; each one of us can say with certainty, "God loves *me.*"

God's greatest concern for us is *not* the pleasures, successes, achievements here in the world because these are not lasting; he may want us to have some of these, but that is not his primary goal for us. God has placed us here as pilgrims, visitors on a trip, a journey; we are on our way *home.* As we travel this journey, God watches over us with concern; there are many pitfalls, evils, enemies who want to steer us away from the way *home: heaven.*

God's love is the reason he created us; we are made for heaven, which is why we were made "in the image and likeness of God," not physically because God is spirit. But our souls, the supernatural souls, are spirits like God.

That kind of *love* that God has for us is *agape.* However, our God also wants to be our friend. God wants to share our *friendship in a love relationship, but that is philia, friendship between equals!* Now the vast difference between the Creator, God, and his creatures, us, is too vast for any imaginable friendship of equals, of sharing sameness of life, of mutual affections. God remains inaccessible to us; he is a divine being, above any being that we can even begin to understand.

Of course, God has a plan for us men, one that he gives only to mankind. He freely offers a way to lift us up to his level of divinity! This is so that we can experience a *philia* relationship, a love relationship between equals. Jesus's birth, death, resurrection made this possible. He gives us the gift of *grace,* which enables us to live in a close, intimate friendship with him. He has made his resting place *in our soul* when we are in a state of grace! God offers us this love relationship. Jesus provides all of this through his church and through a close relationship with him.

Our love for God is usually *not* accompanied by *feelings of love;* sometimes God will give us the gift of the sentiment of love to console us, to help us to remain faithful on our journey back to him. We love God when we follow his commandments and his will for us.

Our love for God is shown by deeds, not feelings. We acknowledge him as our Creator to whom we owe our life, our continued sustenance daily. We owe him our total loyalty. We are loyal lovers of God when we live each day doing our best to get close to Jesus in his humanity. He is our God, our Savior, and our Friend, who shows us the way *home*. Jesus told the disciples, as recorded in John 14:6, that *he is the way, the truth, the life*. He told us that no one could come to the Father except through him, Jesus. Our daily contact with God, with Jesus, through our prayers, is especially important.

A *philia* friendship requires that this love relationship be reciprocal. God gives us his unconditional love and his blessings in our natural state. God freely gives us supernatural life, which we received at our baptism, and he gives us his grace so that we can share his divine life. If we are to remain in a friendship with God, a *philia* relationship, we must work at conforming ourselves to God's will so that we can be like him. For our part in this relationship, we must strive to follow Jesus's teachings; he came to teach us how to be in a love relationship with God, who loves us unconditionally. This love of God may be the only really unconditional love we will ever know in this earthly life. Jesus (God and Man) tells us, as recorded in John 15:14, that we are his friends if we do as he commanded.

There, we have it. If we would be in a relationship with God, through Jesus, we will do what God has commanded and what Jesus has taught. This is the way that we would be "equal"; our will would reflect the divine will. Perfect conformity is perfect union with God. This would be a *philia*, love, relationship.

We can choose to decline this love, this friendship with God. The Lord, our God, will continue to unconditionally love us, no matter our decision. This love of God for us is *agape, forever no matter what, whether we love him or not!*

1. Do I have this love for God? Do I desire this? What will I do to attain this love?
2. *Do I remind myself often that to know, to love, to serve God is my Christian vocation!*

Notes:

Chapter 21

Loving the Difficult Ones

ONE SAINT REMARKED, "If I wish to know whether I possess true charity [love], I must examine myself and see if when I speak about any of my neighbors, I am more ready to mention his virtues or his faults." Oops!

Love is not a feeling; love is a decision to do good to another no matter the feelings we have. There are some people whom we have no interest in, no affinity toward; there are some people who have unlovable qualities. We are taught by Jesus the necessity to *love* them. He shows us how and why it is good.

We sometimes have a natural dislike for other people; their personality annoys us, bores us, even angers us. These are the people around with whom we must be especially careful in order to be loving and charitable. There are people whom we always tend to see their faults, to overlook their virtues. In our eyes their faults are magnified; their goodness is minimized.

The love that God demands of us and that Jesus teaches is that charity makes no distinction of people; all people are to be loved because in all we see and love only God.

Love adapts itself to the other people. Love requires us to accommodate ourselves to others, not only in their need, but also in their mentalities and preferences. Some people are wrong, rude, not understanding or caring about us or our needs, our feelings. So why should we bother with them? We must "bother with them," especially if they are regular in our lives, because God condescended to come down to our level as a human person and lived among many such personalities. We remember some of the men and women he chose to live and associate with; Jesus adapted himself totally to the common people of his time. Jesus hid his power, wisdom, and infinite purity to live among us.

We do not adapt ourselves to the desires of people when they want us to conform to anything against the laws of God or the teachings of Jesus. Instead, much of our adapting ourselves to the other person out of love and good will is that we will be asked to condescend to the "other person's state of being." This means we will not insist on our own personal feelings, point of view, preferences; we will instead surrender ourselves to their mentality, tastes, education, and temperament.

Often, what Jesus asks of us is not easy, unless we are perfect in charity as the saints were. For example, we may be asked for something in a tactless way, a commanding tone, or asked for a favor that is difficult for us. Then our resentment, our self-love, flares up. We want to refuse; we find reasons to refuse. In such instances, we may have to do "violence to ourselves" by graciously placing ourselves in the service of that person! We may have to smother our inner rebellion, but we must help *all others* to carry their burdens, fulfill their tasks and duties.

The Lord asks us to work at understanding others, although they may never try to understand us. The Lord asks us to serve others, care for others, even though they will probably never do the same for us. We are asked to make life pleasant for all those around us no matter how they and others treat us. We do this out of the largeness of our heart because we love God, and he loves us, and them too! The more we give to others, the more God gives us joy and peace so that we have a reward from him, if not from others. The saints tell us that the more we do for others, the happier we will be.

Loving one another is not only in performing heroic deeds. Most often, it is in everyday opportunities, like a *smile, a compliment, a word of encouragement, a thank you, good advice, holding back an angry remark, visiting a sick friend or relative, a telephone call to a lonely person.* These acts are especially important and appropriate for us to use toward those whom the Lord has placed nearest to us; these are the ones with whom we must sometimes struggle the most in order to see Christ in each of them.

One holy man has told us that our greatest treasure is the person who has a need for us; the needy person is the fragile treasure God has placed in our care. And we are told by other holy people that the measure of our charitable acts, patience, forgiveness, and kindness toward others is the measure of our love for God!

1. How much do I love God? I can tell by how much I love the person I want to love least.
2. What am I willing to do? I will plan.
3. I will continue to study Scripture to learn how Jesus loved the unlovable in his life.

Notes:

Chapter 22

Importance of Self-Knowledge

THE ANCIENT GREEKS wrote the maxim "Know thyself" on their temple entrances. Socrates, a famous Greek philosopher, felt that it was foolishness to attempt to learn about many irrelevant things when one did not know himself well, that "the unexamined life is not worth living." Benjamin Franklin said that there are three things that are very hard: steel, diamond, and knowing ourselves. Ralph Waldo Emerson, a famous poet, wrote in 1831 the poem "Gnothi Seauton," translated as "Know Thyself," a song of praise to God, living in us and whom we know when we know ourselves.

The importance of knowing ourselves is well-known; the important thing for Christians to know about ourselves is the moral state of our characters. We must know this to ensure that we are going in the right direction in fulfilling our purpose in life: knowing, loving, serving God and others. We must know this because our souls were made in the "image and likeness" of God, and our moral character must be strong and pure to make us more like God. And following God's will for us depends on how well we are living our moral lives through our vocations. And there is only one way to do this.

Father Basil Maturin, in chapter 1 of his 1939 book *Self-Knowledge and Self-Discipline*, states that most of us are profoundly ignorant of our inner world of motives, ignorant of our moral character. Maturin states that "self-knowledge has nothing to do with mere cleverness or intellectual insight, but is largely, if not totally, moral" (p. 8).

Ralph Martin, a professor of theology, states in his book *The Fulfillment of All Desire* (pp. 181–191) that many saints tell us that it is necessary to gain self-knowledge by comparing ourselves to Jesus. Martin too tells us that knowing if we are weak or strong, intelligent or not so, sweet or rude, is not enough if we are to gain self-knowledge and God knowledge.

To know ourselves, our moral character, there is only one standard, one yardstick that we must use. That standard is Jesus, the Second Person of the Trinity. We are created in the "image of God," not in the flesh, but in the spirit, for God is spirit. Jesus (fully Man and fully God) lived in the flesh for thirty-three years to show us by the example of his life and his teachings how to develop our moral character to restore our soul's "image and likeness of God," which had been disfigured by the disobedience of Adam and Eve.

Therefore, it follows that we must know Jesus very well if he is the teacher of our moral lives. The saying "What would Jesus do?" was very popular a few years ago; we saw it everywhere: T-shirts, mugs, jewelry, banners. This fad soon died out, but this truth is still necessary to evaluate our moral life, to find out what is the basis of our actions.

Jesus said, according to John 4:34, that his food (vocation) was to do the will of God the Father. Jesus did this through his life of poverty and anonymity, then through his words and actions as preacher and teacher, his death and resurrection. This was all to teach us, to show us how to conduct our lives. Finally, this vocation of Jesus was to give us the great gift of restoring our soul's ability to again become "the image and likeness of God" which had been lost by Adam and by our own sins.

Jesus fulfilled the vocation that God had given him to accomplish. Now we must accomplish ours; we must become the self-aware disciple of Jesus worthy of the name Christian. We must study Jesus through prayer, Scripture, spiritual readings from holy people, and meditations.

When we know Jesus, we can see how much we are like him or how different we are, as well as the reasons for the differences. Our moral self-knowledge becomes clearer. We make changes as needed.

This is a lifelong process—daily, weekly, monthly, yearly as we honestly and thoroughly search our consciences.

An important question to ask is, "Do I really want to follow Jesus closely?" If we are too afraid, too lazy, too self-absorbed with our own comfortable lives, too selfish to give our lives to serving God and others, we will learn that our moral characters are weak; we may be far from God's will for our eternal souls. Therefore, if we do want to follow Jesus, if we really desire to do God's will so that our soul somewhat mirrors God's image, then we are on a good path. And the more effort we give to our prayer and doing our duties in our daily lives, the more help God will give us. He created us out of love; he wants us to remain on the journey of self-knowledge.

God, generous and merciful, will give us all the support we need in answer to our prayers for help. The more effort we give to our prayers and doing our duties in our daily life, the more help God will give us. He created us out of love; he wants us to remain in his love. Therefore, when we fail to examine ourselves well in terms of following Jesus or we fail to follow our good resolutions, we damage our moral character. But God will lift us up, forgiving us for what we have done or have failed to do when we sorrowfully ask him. He will help us, again and again, to restore our distorted "soul's image."

1. Is there anything that I do or not do that is contrary to what Jesus would have me do or not do? Do I want to change? What will I do to make these changes? Is that already in my plans?

2. I will study Scripture to help me examine my conscience to gain self-knowledge.

Notes:

Chapter 23

God's Fire of Love

FOR US CHRISTIANS, it is interesting and informative to study how God used fire as a symbol of his love in the Old Testament. And we read in Luke 12:49 that Jesus told his disciples that he came to cast fire upon the whole earth! What did he mean? And then Jesus gave us, his followers, the command to follow him in casting fire over the whole earth. We learn that this fire is love and how it is spread.

In the history of God's interaction with his people, fire has always been important. Fire has always been a symbol of God's love for man. In Genesis 3:24, after God had expelled Adam and Eve from paradise, he placed cherubim with a fiery sword to guard the tree of life. When God first spoke to Moses to commission him to lead the Israelites out of Egypt, he spoke to Moses in a burning, fiery bush; this is recorded in Exodus 3:2. We are told in Exodus 13:21–22 that after the Israelites left Egypt, God led them with a column of cloud during the day and a column of fire at night. In Isaiah 6:6–7, an angel touched Isaiah's lips with a fiery coal to cleanse him from all sins so that he, Isaiah, could do God's work—calling the people to repent of their sins and to return to God, to follow his commandments.

Jesus came to repair the damage caused by the original sin from Adam; he did that by the fire of his love. Only God could repair the damage done by sin; so Jesus, the Son of God, took our humanity unto himself, out of love for us, to give us the opportunity to again have a love relationship with God. Jesus came with the wish to fulfill a mission given to him by God the Father. Therefore, he was anxious to accomplish these tasks: reopen paradise, give us a new religion, send the Holy Spirit to teach us, give us his teachings and his new commandment (love your neighbor as yourself), establish the Holy Eucharist, establish the way to physically remain with us until the end of time.

What does this mean to us? The New American Bible translates in Matthew 28:18–20 Jesus's command to the eleven apostles after his resurrection. This is what he said, "All power in heaven and on earth has been given to me. Go, therefore, and make disciples of all nations, baptizing them in the name of the Father, and of the Son, and of the Holy Spirit, teaching them to observe all that I have commanded you. And behold, I am with you always, until the end of the age."

No, we are not the apostles, but we are followers of Christ, Christians; and our task is to do our part in fulfilling all that Jesus has commanded. Jesus wants us to be personally "on fire" with love for him. And with this love, we must "pass it on"; love calls for love returned. How do we ignite the fire of our love for Jesus? Daily, for him, we serve others gladly. We give up our own plans to accommodate others. We mortify our senses by giving up little pleasures. We do distasteful tasks before those tasks that we like. We talk to him all day, asking for help and thanking him. We offer all of our days for his glory and for the reparation of our sins and those of the whole world. In this way, our hearts and our souls will be blazing with love! Surely, it will warm others!

Jesus loves every soul with no exception! This love that we have will ignite the love of Jesus in other souls. How? Our fire of love for God will manifest itself in the desire to have every soul know and love him. Our love will spill over to include those close to us, where in words, in deeds, in examples, others will feel the flames, even though it may be felt only as an ember. (A blazing fire can be started by a spark.)

We must give every person we encounter something of the love of God. It may be a great service, a small favor; it may be a smile, a friendly word, a helping hand. It may be a silent prayer for someone because of what we see or hear or feel that they need: they may never know that we have prayed for them. This silent prayer is very important when others hurt us, anger us, irritate us. The Holy Spirit will use every effort, small or large, to fan the flames of love. This is setting the world on fire for the love of God, one person, one deed at a time!

The saints and other holy people remind us that the "fire of love of God" has nearly died out upon the earth today! We are experiencing the attempted destruction of our Christian religion, which is the vessel holding the fire of Christ's love for God and God's love for us! We are the flame carrier; it is up to us to keep it burning.

1. What can I do to stir up the "flames of love for God," first in myself, then in others? Will the resolutions that I have made in my plans accomplish this?

2. I can always pray, pray, pray for the world; I can beg the Holy Spirit to show us, me, what I can do, besides what I am already doing, to help this poor world.

3. I will continue to study Scripture.

Notes:

Chapter 24

To Love Is Often Difficult

JESUS ALWAYS WRAPPED everyone, even sinners, especially sinners, in blankets of love and protection. We must do the same as followers of Jesus. Jesus forbids us, as does God the Father, to throw "trash, garbage," onto others through words as well as our actions. We are to cherish others as they did.

We read in Psalm 42:1–4, "Here is my servant whom I uphold, my chosen one with whom I am pleased, Upon whom I have put my spirit; … A bruised reed he shall not break, and a smoldering wick he shall not quench, Until he establishes justice on the earth." This describes Jesus's gentle, respectful, treatment of others. Jesus did not treat people roughly, rudely, angrily; he did not try to break people's spirit, their pride; he did not embarrass people, except the Pharisees when he was soon to leave the earth. He attempted to have them see their hypocrisy so that they could be saved, as well as the people understanding the Jewish leaders' misguided leadership. (See Matthew 23:13–27.)

In Matthew 12:15–21, the writer quotes the words of Psalm 42 to indicate that these words apply to Jesus, his meekness, his not wanting to get into arguments with the Pharisees, who wanted to put him to death. (Jesus chose the time when he was to allow them to crucify him.) Jesus continued to preach and heal, but he asked the people not to make this known. He did not want to call attention to the failings of the Jewish leaders. He wanted others to hear his teachings of the love of God for us and that the kingdom of God had arrived with him.

In the Gospel of John 10, we read the parable of Jesus comparing himself to the good shepherd who takes tender, loving care of each one of his sheep. Jesus guards and protects his flock (us); he knows each one of us by name. He covers each one of us, saints and sinners, with a *"mantle or blanket of love, care, concern, protection."*

One aspect of our following the teaching of Jesus, love your neighbor as yourself, is too often ignored, not taken seriously. "Yeah, yeah, I know I must not gossip about others, but…"

When we discuss the faults, failings, sins of others, we lessen the listener's opinion of the person we are talking about. It is throwing trash on this person's esteem, which we have no right to do. It is lowering that person's reputation. He is one whom we are mandated to love, cherish, protect as one of God's children. God is willingly giving everyone his love and mercy; so should we. Instead of talking about the faults, failings, sins of others, we are commanded to "hide these" as we "hide our own faults, failings, sins." We are to cover everyone with a cloak of respect. We too may have had times of weakness and have sinned; we may have had areas where we were weak in courage, in integrity, in strength of character. We may have been "nearly broken," and "our flame of spiritual, mental, physical fire" was very low"! Hopefully, no one contributed to our brokenness, our feeling of loneliness. Hopefully, no one threw the "trash of discouragement, blame, criticism" on us! Hopefully, someone covered us with a blanket of care, love, protection, support!

In one meditation in *Divine Intimacy*, a well-known and loved book of daily meditation by Father Gabriel, we are advised not to talk about others. We are told not to talk about even those whose poor, sinful behavior is widely known, even if we are not adding any other facts to the situation! We are to "love this person" in spite of tremendous wrongdoing because he is God's child, the work of God's hands. (Love the sinner; hate the sin!) Sometimes, or oftentimes, this is not possible for us to do without God giving us the supernatural ability to do so; we must pray, beg for this grace!

And there is another benefit from which we can all benefit. We are told in Proverbs 10:12 that charity covers many sins. Some of our sins can be erased now by our protecting others from the exposure of their sins and faults!

1. The habit of repeating "bad news" of the day and about others is difficult to change. I will pray for God's grace to help me. I will put this into my plans, my resolutions.

2. There are certain people whom I often "trash." I must be especially careful here.

3. I will read the Scriptures given.

Notes:

Chapter 25

Deadly Demonic Activities

CHRISTIANITY IN THE Western world is besieged by symptoms labeled by theologians of both Catholic and Protestant churches as apathy, boredom, indifference, passivity, and purposelessness. The twenty-first *century appears to be a make-or-break* period for Christianity in the West because too many of us don't care enough to live Christianity well, much less do we want to evangelize our world to Christianity.

We Christians need to understand the causes, dangers, symptoms, remedies of the demonic activities now as reflected in the great apathy and indifference toward God that has infected our Western culture. We want to learn this to save our own souls and our Christian religion for future generations.

First, we have the responsibilities to learn to know, love, and serve God to be happy with him forever; God created each one of us for that purpose. Jesus, together with the Holy Spirit, is the one who teaches us the love of God for us and our love for God.

"The demon of acedia also called the 'noonday devil' is the most oppressive of all demons," so said Evagrius of Pontus, who lived in the years 345–399! He was describing the monks in the desert who were tempted at noontime because they were hot, tired, getting bored with their "work" of solitude, prayer, mortification. Let us explore, as twenty-first-century Christians, how this "noonday devil" affects us who do not live in a desert or in a monastery. We are told that this devil and others are using us to destroy Christianity, the religion that was and is the cause of the greatest civilization on the face of the earth.

The world and demons like acedia attempt to destroy or severely wound the central message from God, who told us, "I love you, and I want you to be happy here and forever." These enemies of Christ, and of us, have succeeded well because too many of us do not know or believe the radical idea that Jesus came to teach us: God loves me more than any other being can love me now, just as I am. Really grasping this message gives us the meaning of our life and gives us a firm eternal goal: to know, love, serve God and thus have peace and joy forever.

If we have lost, or have never known, the central meaning of our lives, then what? A moral life, as taught by Christianity, is vitally important in achieving the goal, the central purpose of our lives (to know, love, serve God). The world today, with the help of demons, broadcasts loud and clear a dangerous, deadly message. This message comes from many institutions such as the media and many other professions. They tell us that the morals and values of Christianity are foolish, nonsense. (Without the belief in the purpose for which God created us, what is the meaning of our lives?) Is this the cause of "midlife crisis"? Unstable in marital crisis? Rampant disobedience? Mob excitement? Addiction? Suicide? Unhealthy, inappropriate relationships?

For many of us, after we have experienced many of the distractions and false claims of the world, we ask, sometimes or oftentimes, "Is this all there is to my life?" If we have had or have now this feeling, it could mean we have lost or never really understood the purpose of our lives.

Therefore, the evil of not knowing and accepting the purpose for which we were created has kept many Christians from a vigorous and active practice of the religion that Jesus established for us to achieve God's desire for us: the peace and joy that comes with a sense of purpose, the achievement of unity with God.

Acedia and other dangerous evils that the world embraces have caused many of us to reject God, to make, unknowingly, a contract with Satan, who promises wealth, power, and unlimited pleasures.

The result of this pact with the devil produces no lasting joy and peace; instead, we see division, violence, sadness, and depression. One person, quoted in *The Noonday Devil* by J. C. Nault, page 110, remarked, "We possess everything, but we do not have God. We have power, but we have lost meaning. Our society [which] is oozing with anxiety… is going to disappear." Many of us are in that number; we may have "sold our souls," albeit unknowingly, have sinned seriously, or not so seriously. We may have been apathetic, lazy, indifferent toward the practice our Christian Faith.

Now our world needs each one of us to experience a deep conversion, a deep understanding of the importance of each one of us to stem the tide of paganism (unbelief in Christianity's value) to which our world is racing. We must learn well, then practice our faith; we must learn how the devil and the world are defeating us. Only then, when we walk the Christian path, can we talk honestly the Christian talk!

The author and abbot Jean-Charles Nault summarizes well the means and the happy result of defeating acedia and other such enemies on page 202 of his book *The Noonday Devil*. He says that this "demon… can be vanquished only by accepting the love of God and the sublimity of our vocation, which, in turn gives rise to the joy of true Christian freedom."

1. I will often reflect on the purpose of my life and how I have succeeded or have failed.
2. I will often reflect on how I have failed or succeeded in following the plans and the resolutions that I have previously made.

Notes:

Chapter 26

The Great Christian Paradox

JESUS TELLS US, as seen in Matthew 10:39, that the person who finds his life and then loses his life for Jesus's sake, will find it again. What does Jesus mean "to lose my life to find it"? This is a paradoxical statement; this means that some part of this statement seems to contradict the rest of the sentence.

How can we make sense of this? This is the great paradox found in Christianity, as told by Saint Paul in 1 Corinthians 1:23: "A stumbling block for Jews" can be a stumbling block for us Christians today, as it was since the beginning of Jesus's religion. An unpopular, hard-to-digest requirement is that to lose our life and regain it is radical and requires striving for holiness. How is this possible?

A basic tenet of Christianity found in Genesis 1:27 is that we are made in the image and likeness of God, spiritually, not physically; God is spirit. This means that we must be, or rather become, like him to get to where he, God, is; we need to be like God to live in his kingdom both here on earth and when we get to heaven. In 1 Peter 1:15–16, we are told that we must "be holy as He is holy." To be holy like God, therefore, we must know him very well. Who can know God?

Jesus came to show us who God is, how we are to relate to him, and how to be friends with God as his children. Jesus left his Holy Spirit and his church to guide, lead, support us in this life until we get to the next life in eternity. As faithful Christians, we need to want holiness. Do we want that friend-child relationship with God? How do we achieve this?

To grow in holiness so that we can live with him, we must know ourselves well; we must know the unholiness we possess in order to make changes to become holier. The way we learn about ourselves, our moral selves, our character is to compare ourselves to Jesus. Imagine! He is the yardstick used to measure ourselves! We become more and more like Jesus when we know him well and follow him closer and closer. This requires not only studying about Jesus but also knowing him personally.

Knowledge of God, especially Jesus, and self-knowledge usually happen simultaneously and gradually as we grow in our search for God and his kingdom. If we are not searching for God, if we are not journeying to him in a deliberate way, we will never know him or ourselves very well. (We will know ourselves and God completely when we are face-to-face with him, as Paul reminds us in 1 Corinthians 13:12.)

Now comes the paradox. We must first have some self-knowledge; *then we must surrender all of ourselves, our lives, to God!* Before we can freely surrender to God, we must have some self-understanding, for we cannot give what we do not possess. This self-surrender of "all that we are and all that we have" is not a one-time event. As we grow in the knowledge of God, through our relationship with him and the humanity of Jesus, we will also grow in knowledge of ourselves. *Therefore, it will require constant surrendering. We will falter, we will stop, we will start over,* we will struggle. This process is a lifetime project. Christian freedom means the ability to choose God, to choose to search for *holiness,* because this is God's will for us. It is not easy to surrender ourselves to God; an independent streak in our human DNA wants to do as Frank Sinatra once sang, "I did it my way." Another name for this streak of independence is original sin. This proud spirit is a great obstacle to a close relationship with God. *Pride* caused Adam and Eve to disobey and lose paradise for themselves and for us too. Pride, refusal to obey God, caused some angels to become devils.

Our whole life may be an exercise in futility for eternity when we do not surrender ourselves to God for any reason. Jesus asks us, as recorded in Matthew 16:28, "Would it be worthwhile to have everything in this world but lose our place in heaven forever?" This is an eternal choice, a matter of heaven or hell.

1. Every day, I must choose to become more holy by following God's will for my life today, or I can choose to "do my own thing."

2. Often, it is not easy and not fun to choose God's will. I must plan strategies to overcome my resistance. I will continue to study the Scriptures.

Notes:

Chapter 27

Spiritual Parenting

TO EACH ONE of us, God gives great treasures and great responsibilities. God expects us to use our gifts to know, love, and serve him in the place where he has placed us. One gift that is expected of *all of us* is to share the love of God that he gives us. God made us supernatural mothers and fathers of souls! Many souls! Multitudes of souls! God chose us to parent souls, to help him to bring grace to all souls—the souls of those in our family, in our immediate environment, as well as souls through the whole world!

How is it possible that God would use, even need, our participation to give supernatural grace, salvation, a path to heaven, to all souls? What is God's plan? How do we do this? How does this get accomplished?

In the natural world, two of God's creatures, one man and one woman, physically united, can bring forth physical, human life. On the supernatural level, God puts forth the same plan, a union of two. And in the sphere of supernatural activity, God and a human being, either a man or a woman, can unite to help bring forth a supernatural life of grace to another human, physical body. How awesome is that? How is this possible? Catholics know that priests have the super awesome vocation, the power of bringing grace to all men, through the sacraments and through his life sacrificed for us men. But we too are disciples, and in 1 Peter 2:9, he tells us that not only are we the chosen people of God, but we are a "royal priesthood." We are priests too; we can bring grace to souls! The duty, the responsibility, the privilege has been entrusted to us: we are to go out to the whole world to help God bring salvation through his grace. (We can accept this life-giving duty, or we can reject this God-entrusting opportunity.)

How can this spiritual union of God and a humble, made-from-dust human unite? On the human level, the union of man and woman is—or should be—made in love: love for one another, the desire to give one another their whole being, their whole life. It is the same in one's spiritual life. The union of God and man or woman is also the result of love. God loves us; that is the reason he created us, cares for us, keeps our souls alive forever. Now, God cannot make us love him; he waits. His blessings, care, protection are freely given, even if we do not return his love. When we seek God, when we want to love him, we do find him. When we surrender ourselves, our lives, our will, to God, because we know that he is our Creator, our benefactor, we are spiritually *joined* to them, the Trinity, the one God in three Persons: God the Father, Jesus the Son, and the Holy Spirit. *This joining of our souls with God fills us with God's life of grace!* And the more we love God, the more "full of grace" we become; the more grace fills us, we are moved to share this supernatural gift with others.

How does this sharing of grace, the supernatural love of God, happen? How do we distribute our grace? The Virgin Mary, in Luke 1:34, asked the angel Gabriel, who told her that she was to be the mother of the Savior, "How can this be?" for she was not married. The angel told her that it would be done through the work of the Holy Spirit. We ask, "How can this be done?" How can we pass on the grace that God continues to pour into our souls? The answer is the same as the one given Mary; *the Holy Spirit will guide us as to what and how God wants us to help him share his grace with others to redeem their souls. This is how we become spiritual parents.*

Like Mary's "fiat," our saying "yes" to God's love and desire to share in the distribution of his love and grace involves much joy and much work, especially in the forms of prayer and sacrifice. The Lord Jesus asks the same of each of us, as a sacrifice, always doing all what is required of our daily duties in whatever state of life we are: consecrated life, married life, single life. Whatever career, job, profession we are engaged in, we are to do the best that we can. Fulfilling our daily duties and responsibilities well, offering it to God for ourselves and others, is the major means that the Holy Spirit uses to bless those we love, those we care about, those in our surroundings, and the whole world! We do what we are supposed to do well; the Lord takes this "good work" as a gift and distributes it to others! The prayers that we offer, the sacrifices that we wholeheartedly accept in doing our work, in the living of our day—all are means of sharing the gifts of grace that we own from this work. The prayers and sacrifices of spiritual parents are like those of human parents.

The more that we love the Lord, the more we have to give to others, the more fruitful will be our work of bringing God to others, and the more souls God will bring to us—both physically near or faraway. Some we will know; some we will never know until in the next life, where we will meet.

In addition, often, the Holy Spirit asks some of us to use our talents and time to further the kingdom of God beyond the scope of our natural duties. This requires discernment in which the Holy Spirit will aid us. We will be shown what and how the kingdom needs us.

The life of Jesus, the lives of the saints, and the lives of holy people whom we know and live with show that sacrifice is a large part of the spiritual path for all, including spiritual parents. Yet there are no people more joyful, peaceful, happy, energetic than those of us who are filled with the love of God! *We are the light of the world! We are the yeast in the bread, the body of Christ in the church!*

1. I will form the habit of offering to Jesus all my prayers, works, joys, and suffering for all the intentions of his Sacred Heart—the salvation of souls, the reparation of sins, the intentions of my family, friends, the whole world. Jesus will use all my graces to benefit all and more!

2. I will continue to look for opportunities to "pass on the love of Jesus" to others.

3. I will continue to study Scripture to learn of God's Great love for me.

Notes:

Chapter 28

Need of New Pathways
to Body and Brain

HOW MANY NEW Year's resolutions have we made? How many resolutions have lasted a few days, weeks, the whole year? Most of us have not been able or willing to follow through with our plans. Why? Why is it that we often listen to an inspiring talk, lecture, homily that motivates us to want to make some change in our life, but nothing happens? We may have started, but we soon stop; maybe we have never even started the "change." Why? What about a desire to be a more faithful follower of Christ? Have we thought about this at all? Or did we ever have this inspiration, but we did nothing about it? Why? To make serious changes, to form new habits and replace familiar, comfortable habits, poor or sinful habits, is scary and difficult.

The resolution to be a more faithful disciple of Christ is daunting, scary. However, our Lord bids us to change, be converted in many areas of our life, if we are to follow him. Saint Paul tells us in Ephesians 4:22–24 that we must put aside the "old man," our old way of life. He tells us that we must renew the spirit of our mind, put on a new self, a new vessel for the soul. He tells us that our minds (will) must be overhauled. We must follow Christ, not the world (certainly not this culture of the twenty-first century). Saint Paul tells us that our *minds must change; any lasting change in our behavior will come only after our will has fully agreed to the decision.* That is what is needed to convert our lives fully to Christ.

Problems will immediately begin to manifest themselves when we want to make needed changes. Our old self, which is frozen in deep habits, deep ruts, will resist changes. Our will must be *strong to fight, constantly at first,* to break these old habits *by acquiring new habits.* The body and brain pathways will want to continue on the easy road of the old habits. New habits are not easy to acquire; supernatural support can and must help to make this happen for us. This help will be given but only with our continuing necessary hard work.

A further problem that almost always arises involves other people. The world does not want us to change; we will be pressured to remain the same. This objection to our conversion may occur among our own family members, friends, and coworkers because they may be forced to adjust to our changed self. This can be uncomfortable, annoying, even fearful for them.

And everything that we see around us in the media, social media, television, movies—all make it more difficult to remain faithful to our conversion process. Everything we encounter in the world appeals to our senses: ease, comfort, pleasure. The culture encourages freedom from difficulties, discomforts, pain; it even makes it easy for us to escape our responsibilities and duties.

A vital part of the process to change habits, especially at the beginning of our conversion, is to pray *constantly* to God, to Jesus, to the saints, to our guardian angel; we will be assisted. However, we must put all our own efforts to get full support from God. Small efforts equal small results. At all times, but especially at the beginning of our conversion, the support of other people is crucial. Faithful Christians and church groups are vital to continuing our path to God. We must seek this!

The path to renewing our minds is an inside job, a "head" job. Our Lord is not usually asking us to change locations, jobs, friends, family; however, it may be that some of us may have to make these radical changes. Usually, Jesus is asking us to submit our lives to him, wherever we are, and to let him be our guide, our leader. Our resolutions and inspirations will be easier to accomplish with his help.

God will allow us to progress on our new path, conversion, at our own pace, but we must not stop. Maybe slow but sure is okay, but no stopping. And he will bless us with peace and joy now and forever. (But often, it will take time to get to *peace and joy*).

Pope Saint John Paul II, as quoted in Francis Fernandez's *In Conversation with God*, volume 1, page 135, beautifully states the way to change our minds and our lives: "Open the gates wide to Christ. Take the risk of following him... you should come out of your own way of reasoning... leave behind your self-sufficiency, those un-Christian habits... Let all your relationships, activities, feelings, thoughts, be integrated in Him, or so to speak, 'Christified'. I wish... that with Christ you may come to recognize God as the beginning and the end of your existence." May we give an "Amen, I believe," to the pope's wish for us. May we be strong with God's strength and continue our journey to him, overcoming all obstacles and hurdles. Glory to God!

1. I will make a resolution about changing one or more deep-rooted habits that are spiritually and/or physically or mentally destructive.
2. Next, will I make a specific, never general, plan.
3. Then I will begin, knowing that I will fall but rise again, fall and rise, until my body and mind are rerouted to new habits. I will ask, "Lord, help me!"

Notes:

Chapter 29

From Sinner to Saint

IT HAS BEEN noted in the history of Christianity that, very often, great sinners become the church's great saints, leaders, teachers. This can be important to us. Their lives show us God's mercy and goodness. We can gain much by exploring their lives, which show how we can proceed from sin to holiness, from sinner to saint. And this can be done in a short time! So old or young, we can achieve this. The lives of saints give us hope and encouragement to repent and convert our lives because we can see that it is possible.

We remember Saint Paul, dedicated attacker of the new Christian religion, who watched the first Christian martyr, Stephen, being stoned to death, his silence signifying agreement. Then his goal to capture Christians in Damascus and return them in chains was interrupted by Jesus, who struck him off his horse with visions, blindness, instructions. Convinced that Jesus is the Christ, he preached the gospel with courage and fortitude, becoming the Great Apostle of the Gentiles. Saint Paul's writings and teachings found in the New Testament are a "backbone" of Christianity.

Another great Christian saint of early Christianity is Augustine of Hippo, theologian and philosopher, who lived from AD 354 to 430. Augustine converted from a pagan life of excessive worldly pleasure, especially sins of the flesh; his writings are often autobiographical. His contribution to Christianity continues to educate Christians even to this day. His mother, Monica, had prayed for his conversion for years; his conversion evolved slowly. He was not eager to abandon his worldly pleasures; he was afraid that he could not remain pure. But Augustine did change his life with the grace of God, undoubtedly strengthened by his mother's prayers; and he became a giant Christian saint.

The Gospel of Luke 15:11–32 recounts Jesus's parable of the young prodigal (lost) son returning to his father's house after a worldly, sinful life had left him destitute, suffering, starving. He made his way home to his father's house for a place as a servant. (His coming back to his father's house parallels all of us sinners coming home to God.) The young son was welcomed with open arms as a son, not a servant, "wined and dined" with great love and joy; no demands were made of him. This is how our Lord treats us when we return home to him after we have sinned, even after we have sinned seriously.

King David of the Old Testament committed adultery and murder, was forgiven after he repented, but he was severely punished. David was a great sinner and king, but he was greatly loved by God, as we are all loved by him.

Saints Paul and Augustine, after their conversions, spent the rest of their lives thanking God for his goodness, love, and mercy. They found their home in Christianity, Jesus's religion, their holy lives making amends and reparations for their past. It is undoubtedly true that the prodigal son also spent a lifetime thanking his father and making amends for wasting his inheritance in shameful, sinful behavior.

And so it is with us. It appears that when we have deeply offended God, when we have committed serious sins and broken God's commandments, when we come to our senses and realize what we have done, we can be overwhelmed with gratitude and joy at God's forgiveness. This is especially true when we are forgiven in Jesus's sacrament of reconciliation. We who are converted serious sinners are more aware of God's great love and mercy than those of us who have never strayed far away from God by serious sins. Psalm 38:17–18 states it well: "Thus is my bitterness transformed into peace. You have preserved my life from the pit of destruction, When you cast behind your back all my sins." This psalm, attributed to King David, marks the relief and gratitude of all forgiven souls.

We who were by God's grace able to avoid serious sins may have never felt the great relief and gratitude of reconciliation with our Lord that some of us feel. We think of Mary Magdalene, whom Jesus forgave of serious sins, and the great love and devotion she exhibited as a result of this forgiveness. We sinners, all sinners, must pray that Jesus will give us the great grace to follow him closely with love and devotion to rise from our sins—great and small. This is a great gift that only a merciful God can give.

The great sinners turned saints in our Christian history have given us the greatest and best examples of God's mercy, goodness, and love through their conversion stories. Their lives show how true it is that God can use all things to work for good for those who love him, as Paul tells us in Romans 8:28. These great saints show us their frail humanity and their struggles to achieve sainthood. This struggle, falling and rising from sin, is what God expects of us whom he has made in his image. This is the spiritual battle all people are engaged in.

1. From what sins do I fall often? What plans will make to change this?

Notes:

Chapter 30

The Challenge of Unselfishness

MANY PEOPLE IN our Western culture appear to be almost totally self-absorbed and selfish. We see this in the behavior of so many people who disregard others around them; they display rudeness, unkindness, disrespect. They ignore others and display total indifference to the feelings and belongings of other people. It is a sad comment on our culture when we can call so many of us as being narcissistic and sociopathic in behavior; we may not fall completely into this category based on the mental health professional diagnostic chart, but too many of us display these symptoms. This kind of behavior is very contrary to God's laws and Jesus's teachings. In order that we remain peaceful in this kind of environment, we must learn how to respond to others' selfishness; and we definitely need to get rid of our own selfishness.

Much of our popular culture advises us to be solicitous for ourselves first and always. Our society presents as a "right," an entitlement, that we deserve whatever we "want and desire," and that we should have it "now." We are encouraged to be preoccupied with ourselves, our feelings; we are seemingly encouraged and pampered by many institutions and ignorant or devilish people. This selfish attitude is the cause of dissatisfaction and destruction of marriages, workplaces, friendships, communities. This is a major cause of rebellion and anger at our governments and other institutions that cannot satisfy the unfair demands of selfishness.

As Christians, followers of Jesus, we believe that God has placed us in this time and place and situation that he knows is best for us and for those around us. He has especially in mind the "spiritual" best for us and all the people around us. This "best" means that which is helpful to our spiritual journey, which leads us to him in heaven, our true home. And we are to serve him and others here in this time and place (unless the situation we are in is abusive or dangerous).

Our relationship with others must always be based on others' relationship with God; this means that we love and serve and respect others because they are God's creations, his children. And anytime we neglect our relationship with God, the neglect causes us to relate to others, not because of our love for God, but selfishly, we relate to them because of how they affect us. Then we revert to the self-ishness of our flawed nature. (We love them, hate them, like them, dislike them, and treat them in accordance to *our* feelings, not God's feelings.)

It is often difficult to relate to others as Jesus wants us to do; many people are rude, busy, mean, hateful, unlovable. It requires much courage, strength of character, and grace to overcome *our natural feelings* in relating to others who are behaving in these ways. Only God can give us the *heart* to allow us to do the best thing for others. We do not allow others to abuse us, but we must rise above the shortcomings of others with the grace of God and act as Jesus did. We meditate on the Scriptures, which show us how Jesus responded when he was spat upon, scourged, and hung naked upon a cross. When Jesus changes our hearts, we will more easily respond with love to those who disrespect and annoy us, and hopefully, the others will respond by amending their behavior, but maybe not. What matters is our actions.

To be unselfish means we act and react to others with generosity. In order to be able to do this, we must be a firmly committed follower of Jesus, who teaches us how to know, love, and serve God and helps us fulfill our destiny by forgetting ourselves. We will often have to give up our own interests, our own plans, our conveniences, our rights so that we can give ourselves to others for God's sake. In other words, selfishness must not stain our relationships with others, not only with loveable ones, but also with difficult-to-love people. Jesus tells us, as recorded in Matthew 25:40–45, that whatever we do to the least of our brothers, we do to him. The difficult people may be the *least* in our world.

Seems impossible to do! On our own, as Jesus tells us, as recorded in John 15:5, we cannot do anything, much less always act generously, unless we are united to him as a branch (us) to the vine (Jesus). And Paul tells us in Philippians 4:13 that he, Paul, and we, can do all things with Jesus, who strengthens us.

Jesus, no matter how much he was rejected, no matter how tired and hungry he was, never quit giving his "all" to whoever needed him. We, on the other hand, have difficulty letting go of our laziness, comfort-seeking selfishness. Generosity does not seem to be in our DNA.

In President John F. Kennedy's inaugural speech in January 1961, he made a statement that rang in the hearts of all who heard it around the world; it continues to encourage some of us today. The address spoke of man's potential for greatness, challenging us to rise above our selfish self-seeking: it is the same that God asks of us each day. Kennedy said, "My fellow Americans: ask not what your country can do for you; ask what you can do for your country." In other words, we must ask, "What can I do for others?"

1. I will examine my conscience often for acts of selfishness; I will work to amend this tendency.
2. I will make a conscious decision to be more generous; I can do this with words, actions, like compliments, thanks for things done for us, small tokens of appreciation.
3. I will continue to study Scriptures to strengthen my love for God and others in my world.

Notes:

Chapter 31

Tools for Our Spiritual Journey Home

WE HAVE BEEN told in several instances in Scripture that our souls are made in the image of God. We are to keep this image of God clean and pure; we are to be "holy and perfect as he is holy." God helps us to be able to do this; he provides what we need as we Christians make progress in our pilgrimage to our Father's house, our final home. We are like the lepers in Matthew 8:2, who asked Jesus to make them clean. We too must be "clean of the illness of sin." Jesus is our physician as he tells us, as recorded in Matthew 9:12, that he is the doctor who will heal us. Therefore, we struggle daily to remain clean and pure, relying on Jesus, who will give us the "medicines" we need to be like him and our Father.

Jesus provides the tools we need in order to stay "clean of heart" as we travel home. These tools are opportunities to and for us to perform, along with our prayers and the suffering we encounter in our daily lives.

We give *care and protection* for all those who are ours; all their needs are ours to fill as much as we can. This opportunity to serve is one of the best tools in our toolbox. Doing well and willingly our duties and serving others is a means to becoming holy and perfect.

Sometimes we must struggle against the *tide of dehumanization* of certain individuals in our hard-hearted culture: the unborn, the elderly, the disabled, especially the mentally challenged, the severely ill, and others who are not like us in any way. They are marginalized individuals because *they are deemed useless by our pagan culture.* We must fight against this evil in our society. We must continue to vigorously promote the dignity of all of God's children, made in "his likeness." This "fight" we participate in through much prayer and actions when we have the opportunity is a protection for others and is a means for us to be "like Jesus," helping the weaker, the least, of our brothers and sisters.

There are other spiritual obligations (and tools) the Christian must use. It is our duty to *correct those in error* in a respectful and charitable manner when the opportunity is before us. This responsibility is sometimes difficult and unpleasant because many will take offense when they are confronted. However, it is sometimes our obligation to do this correction in the best way we can. If we are in a close relationship with the Holy Spirit, he will give us the wisdom and helpful words to use when we pray to him for help. This service of correcting others provides a great service to our own souls as well as to the others' souls.

Another tool to use and a duty to fulfill is *to teach others* about our religion. Certainly, our lives need to be good examples of true Christianity; however, we may often have the opportunity and the responsibility to teach some aspect of Christianity to those who are in ignorance of God and his laws and decrees, about Christ Jesus and his religion, Christianity. Ignorance is one of the greatest tools that Satan has used in the last several decades to wound Christianity and mislead many away from God. The devil's tactic, which he used with Adam and Eve and which still works with many, many of us, is to deceive us with arguments like "God doesn't really mean that. That religion stuff is just to scare us with the idea of hell." In a recent homily in a mass streamed on EWTN, one priest stated that he found in the Gospel of Matthew alone seventy references to the consequence of unrepented sins, causing one to enter hell instead of heaven. This same priest quoted a current theologian who stated that today's world has turned upside down a passage from Matthew 7:13 where Jesus says, "For wide is the gate and broad is the road that leads to destruction... and many follow it. Enter through the narrow gate that leads to life… and few find it." The world and the devil try to trick us with the opposite: they tell us that there are just a few who will find perdition (hell). Scripture in the Old Testament also warns us against the dangers of ignorance. In Hosea 4:6, the prophet says that God complains that his people are perishing from lack of knowledge. Therefore, some of us who have the ability and the opportunity to teach in classes, workshops, and other such settings must do so. We are required to spread God's teachings. The fact that hell does exist is only one truth we must help our people (and God's) gain knowledge of.

Another opportunity and tool all of us Christians have is *to counsel, to guide, to advise those who ask us, those who seek help from us.* (Unwanted advice can be very detrimental to Christianity; caution and discernment must be used.) However, many of us have been, will be, in situations in which we could enlighten others about our Christian faith. Often, topics brought into conversations need our Christian viewpoint to clarify or inform some point about the subject being discussed. We Christians need to study, to know our faith well, to be informed about current issues in the culture. This knowledge is a great gift for us and others; opportunities must not be missed because of our own ignorance.

We also use the opportunities *to console those who are suffering* from physical pain, emotional and mental pain, any grieving that they are experiencing. Just lending emotional care when we can do nothing else is a great blessing for others; it prevents them from feeling alone in their pain. (And how fortunate we are when we have someone who shares our suffering.)

The major tool in the arsenal of weapons for the battles we daily encounter on our spiritual journey is one that all of us can and must use often daily, constantly: *prayer.* We pray for the living and the dead. We pray when we are young and old; we pray when we are healthy and vibrant or weak and ill. These conversations with God, prayer, are what give us the strength to bear and overcome temptations and discouragement and to survive our constant falling and rising and starting over, again and again and again, all of our lives. These prayers are what are most desperately needed.

The tools we have for our spiritual battles are those opportunities that God sends to all of us our entire lives. It has been said that Jesus told Catherine of Siena that temptations (hardships) are not a sign of anger or hatred for us but tests to strength our virtues. As Saint Paul tells us in Corinthians 10:13, God will not test us beyond our strength while we are on the way to him, our Father in heaven.

1. Do I recognize the opportunities to help and support others are also meant to benefit me? I will often reflect on those trials I encounter as opportunities for me.

2. I will plan opportunities to help others for their own benefit and mine too.

3. I will study the Scriptures to increase my knowledge of God and my love for him.

Notes:

Chapter 32

_____

Religion of Mercy

THE AUTHOR OF *Divine Mercy*, Father Gabriel, has a beautiful definition of *mercy*; he says, "Mercy is love bending over misery to relieve it, to redeem it, to raise it up to himself." Luke 7:2 records for us how Jesus came to show us his and God the Father's mercy and compassion for all of us who are suffering in any and all ways. He did this in the actions he took to alleviate pain, suffering, even death; he also showed the value of mercy and compassion in giving us many parables, which he used to exemplify this mercy.

Therefore, we Christians, followers of Jesus, are obligated to learn that if we want mercy, we must be merciful. We must learn about Jesus's mercy toward all he met; we must provide the mercy that is needed in situations we are confronted with because we are to do his work; it is our duty. And we must learn how to "soften our hard hearts" so that we can more easily do this work.

Jesus has told us in several ways, but especially in a part of the Our Father prayer, that the amount of mercy we will receive is the amount we first give to others. The prayer says, "Forgive us our trespasses as we forgive those who trespass against us;" and when Peter asked Jesus whether he should forgive someone seven times for an offense, Jesus told Peter, as written in the Gospel of Matthew 18:21–22, "No; seventy times seven." This amount designates an unlimited number of times. The amount of mercy that God can give us is the amount that our heart has given to others; it appears that the amount we give is our heart's capacity for giving mercy, and Jesus tells us that it is also our capacity for receiving mercy. We cannot give if we do not receive; we cannot receive if we cannot give! A "small heart is closed, hard as a rock." We must act "as if" we have a large, soft heart, even though we do not "feel" merciful. And we will pray, as we act that God will soften and enlarge this heart of ours; he is the only one who can. (Incidentally, this "act as if" is also a twelve-step advice for those who want to recovery from addictions.)

We Christians have a plan for receiving great mercy from God to alleviate our great needs. We must expand our hearts' ability to give and receive this beautiful virtue. The first requisite for God's great mercy to reach us is that we must recognize and acknowledge our sins and faults. If we are like the Pharisees, who thought of themselves as "not so bad," we cannot absorb God's mercy because we do not believe that we need mercy. We believe ourselves, very wrongly, that we are not great sinners, or sinners at all. Each one of us was born with original sin inherited from Adam; all of us have sinned. No one ever, even the greatest saints, except Jesus and Mary, was "full of grace"; only they were not in need of mercy from God the Father.

How can we realize our sinfulness and need of God's constant mercy? When we measure ourselves by the standards that Jesus set for us by his words and his life and actions, we will know that we need mercy. When we study Jesus's life, however, we also develop confidence in God's great mercy! The more we realize Jesus's mercy toward us, the more the Holy Spirit will teach us what we lack and how to expand our hearts and souls to accept God's mercy and love and to be able to give this mercy and love to others! Jesus's entire life showed us his mercy toward all, even his executioners.

The first recipients of our mercy must be those who are closest to us, and these are the ones we need to give more mercy to and, hopefully, we will receive most mercy from. Forgiveness is the great gift of mercy others can give us and we can give them; so many hurts, pains, sufferings are inflicted by those whom we love and who love us and whom we hurt also. Mercy and love forget, overlook, pay little attention to hurts that those we love exhibit toward us. This is what God does. Jesus's entire life showed us his mercy toward all, even his executioners; he said, dying on the cross, "Father, forgive them, they know not what they do."

Jesus's mercy was intertwined with his constant prayers, conversations with the Father. This gave him the power, the ability to show God's merciful love. This is what we Christians must copy from Jesus's life. Our religion must be a constant raising of our hearts and minds to God, to Jesus, and to the Holy Spirit to petition for our needs, to ask for forgiveness, to praise and thank them for their love and mercy.

1. I will examine my days' activities to look for the mercy I have shown and for that which I have omitted.

2. I will reflect upon the mercy I have received from God and others.

3. I will continue to mediate on Scripture to learn more about mercy and my need to give and to receive this great gift.

Notes:

Chapter 33

Eternal Decisions

NOTHING IS MORE destructive for us than to be of "two minds" about any situation in which we are unable or unwilling to make a decision and "move on." We cannot proceed. We feel stuck. We suffer mental and often physical pain, anxiety, and confusion when our reason and our will cannot or will not make a firm decision in daily life situations. One holy person said that at times like these, it feels like we are walking with one foot on the sidewalk and the other in a ditch!

This is the cause of our saying and hearing from others, "This is driving me crazy." We can continue the turmoil when we second-guess our decisions; we continue the chaos when we begin thinking, *I should have...* or *I should not have...* This can be a common problem for some of us.

There is an important decision we Christians must make, not only for our sanity and peace of mind now, but because this decision will be important into eternity. This mindset will affect our eternal salvation or damnation. Will we make a firm decision to be a true, firm follower of Christ, a true Christian? When we cannot make a firm decision to follow Jesus, to choose to live for God alone, our emotional, mental, even physical lives now may be deeply affected. Also, because we live closely with and around others, our choices affect them also, sometimes directly, sometimes indirectly, as by our examples. Therefore, we need to know why our best decisions should be living well the teachings of Jesus, understanding what keeps us from doing this and knowing what other choices (albeit poor ones) some of us choose.

In Matthew 6:24, Jesus tells us that we Christians cannot serve two masters in this life, or we will end up with love for one and hatred for the other. We can choose as the master of our lives God and his will for us. Or we can choose our own selves as the master because we believe that we do not really need God; we can take care of ourselves. There is a constant spiritual struggle for mastery between our ego, the natural man who strives for comfort, pleasure, and power, and the spiritual man, striving for obedience to God and his will. Saint Paul beautifully describes this struggle in Romans 7:15: "For I do not do the good I want, but I do the evil I do not want."

Father Gabriel of St. Mary Magdalene's book *Divine Intimacy*, page 853, gives us a beautiful definition of the virtue of *simplicity*, which is also defined as *unity*, necessary for mental and spiritual well-being. He says, "Simplicity... embracing man's whole moral life and reducing it to unity... excludes every form of duplicity and complication stemming from egoism, self-love, or attachment to self and to creatures; hence it impels the soul in one direction only: to God, to live for Him, to please Him, and to give glory to Him."

Choosing God's mastery, not our little egos is a *life decision, a life plan.* This decision not only helps us unify our emotional, mental, and spiritual lives, but unifies us with God. God made us to know, love, and serve him in this life, to be happy here and forever with him. Our Christian *life plan*, therefore, is one that puts God first; our own plans, our self-love, is then subjected to God's will for us. Unity and salvation is the result.

We will not always succeed in following God's will, as Saint Paul told us about his own life. We will fail, sometimes badly, sometimes very often. We can often move away from God; he never leaves us. When we sincerely regret our falls, our sins, and begin to rise again to walk in obedience, God forgives us immediately, readily, graciously. This choice to surrender our lives to God is very difficult at times because we often must give up what we would prefer to do or to have.

This involves sacrifices, discipline, the cross. And it is not a "one time only" choice; it is constantly, daily, choosing God.

There are other choices that are possible, although less salvific. (1) We Christians can choose to live "fragmented" Christian lives, choosing to follow Christ in some areas but not in others; we can be "cafeteria Christians," who pick and choose the teachings, the commandments we choose to follow, and those we disregard. We can become "settled" morally, emotionally, spiritually into that place with no more conflict and confusion. (2) We can decide to follow our own will, leave God out of our lives. This choice of not choosing God as master in any part of our lives can also become "settled," frozen; then there is no chaos or confusion. However, these are two very dangerous positions in which to place ourselves; not being in confusion, not feeling any "pain" of conflict, can mean that not only are we not in close union with Christ, but we may be on a path that is not eternally bound for heaven; Scripture repeatedly tells us this truth.

Thanks be to God that we can "change our minds" at any given moment while there is still life in us. God will accept us joyfully even at the last minute; hopefully, we will be able to have this opportunity if we are not in perfect unity with him.

The decision to live God's purpose for us, to know, love, serve him, makes for peace and joy. Living not to please ourselves or the devil or the world not only pleases God but benefits us, those we love, everyone in the church, and the whole world. The saints tell us that by a mystery of God, all the world will reap the "good" we do through our unity with him because all Christians are part of the community of saints! We give thanks to God!

1. Have I surrendered my life to God? I will continually meditate on this.
2. There are areas of my life that I have kept to myself rather than give to him; I will pray that God help me change these.
3. I will continue to work on the plans that I have already made.

Notes:

Chapter 34

The Work of Prayer

WHEN JESUS'S APOSTLES asked him to teach them to pray, as recorded in Luke 11:1, Jesus taught them the Our Father prayer. Almost every Christian knows that prayer; many of us pray this prayer daily and often especially in public, vocal praying. We have learned the words of the Our Father *probably as young children; many little children know these words.*

But do we know how to pray this prayer and other prayers? Many of us do not know how to pray, or do not practice what we do know; we can be like the little children who recite the words but have no clue as to what they are saying. *Prayer is hard work!* There are methods, ways to pray and to be really communicating with God; there are steps we can take.

In Matthew 6:6, Jesus tells us that we are to pray in *secret*. This means in a private place, alone; this also means that we pray in our *heart of hearts*, our inner self, our mental self. Whether we are alone or in a crowd, we focus our attention on the God whom we are talking to. Genuine *prayer is hard work*. We must remain vigilant about remaining in God's presence while we are praying. If we do not do this, our prayer is just a recitation of words—meaningless because our lips say the words but our thoughts and imagination, our heart, are somewhere else. When we find ourselves being distracted, we gently bring ourselves back to God. We go on as though we were never distracted! God understands this; this returning to God is good. *Prayer is hard work!*

To stay focused, which is not always easy, we can follow one of two methods. One, we can focus on the words of the prayer; by paying attention to the words and phrases, we remain with God. We are addressing words, ideas, feelings to him. Another method of focusing in prayer is to give God our total attention. We image him in whatever way we want; we can see him standing before us, smiling at us, as an infant, on the cross, with his apostles, with his mother, Mary. As we place all our attention on looking at him, Jesus or God the Father, the words of the prayers are a background for recitation of praise or thanksgiving or petition. We pay attention to our God, not to words; this is both verbal and mental prayer.

In Luke 18:1, Jesus tells us to pray unceasingly, untiringly. This we can do all day long using short vocal prayers. We can raise our thoughts, our sight, up to God without words, with trust and love. We can silently ask him for what we and others need; we can thank him for graces and blessings, even for the troubles and sufferings because we know that he allows all that happens, even suffering, for our good and the good of others. We may never in this life know why God has allowed tragedies and suffering, but we trust him because he loves us.

Our church has a treasure of traditional prayers, poems, and hymns composed by saints and other holy people, which are beautiful vocal and mental prayers prayed by generations of devout Christians. Many are beautiful prayers addressed to Mary, the mother of God, to the saints, the angels, especially our own guardian angel. We ask them to intercede for us. We know they are with God and have access to him constantly; therefore, we ask for their help.

Without the grace from God, it is impossible to keep continual attention to our prayer; we need to ask for this grace. One beneficial way we can constantly pray is for us to address God in short vocal or mental prayers from the time we are getting dressed in the morning until the time we fall asleep. These prayers are indispensable for keeping God present to us the entire day. The saints have told us and shown us through their lives that the secret of "fruitful Christian lives" is the fact they pray often, sometimes continuously. Holy people *have always told us that the strength to make progress in our journey back home to God* and to fulfill the duties of our vocations lies in our prayer life. *Prayer is beautiful in the sight* of God! Praying is difficult sometimes, but joyful.

It has been said that Blessed Saint André Bessette, called Montreal's Miracle Worker, canonized in 2010, sat for hours before the Blessed Sacrament, both day and night. People would asked him, "What are you doing all that time"? His answer: "I look at God and God looks at me." Being with God is what matters.

1. I realize that praying is hard work; it is not a habit for me. I will begin today.

2. I will practice saying the Our Father and other prayers in the two methods given in this lesson.

Notes:

Chapter 35

Carriers of God's Kingdom

RECORDED IN LUKE 17:21, Jesus says, "The kingdom of God is within you." What does this mean? If it means that the kingdom of God is within our bodies, our own persons, how is this possible? It certainly means that this is an awesome mystery and awesome responsibility. We examine; we study this mystery.

Jesus left this world as a man, ascended into heaven, leaving eleven ignorant, scared, weak men around one lone woman, Mary. And he gave them the command to evangelize the whole world; they, and we, were to spread his Gospel of the good news to the ends of the earth. Realistically, logically, in the world's reasoning, this was not possible. But he sent the Holy Spirit, who instilled in them vitality, energy, boldness, wisdom, knowledge, strength, and courage. Within a few years, this small nucleus had spread throughout the mighty pagan Roman Empire.

This spread of Christianity came about when everyone whom they had baptized received, as we all did, the seed of God's grace, *sanctifying grace*, a gift from God. As each baptized person *nurtured* this seed of grace, it grew stronger and stronger. The early Christians grew stronger in their knowledge and love of Jesus; they spread this love by loving and serving those around them. Those whom they were in contact with became enthusiastic about Jesus and his new religion, Christianity; they were converted. The church grew, one person at a time.

And so it still is today. People, baptized or not, do not usually seek conversion, or have a lasting conversion, to a religion. Conversion is turning one's life to a person, Jesus Christ! We who are baptized were given the seed of sanctifying grace when we received the sacrament of baptism; God continues to pour grace into our souls as we follow Jesus. A basic teaching of Christianity is that God sends us inspirations, opportunities, and events, which helps us grow in our interior lives. When we, filled with the Holy Spirit, give (consecrate) our whole life, our entire body and soul, to our God to benefit ourselves and others, he wholeheartedly accepts us—as we are! Then, the Father, the Son, and the Holy Spirit come and dwell in our souls. They remain with and in us, which is now their kingdom, as we love and serve and glorify them. The kingdom of God is within each of us. Is that not a great responsibility?

The parable of the mustard seed, as recorded in Matthew 13:31–32, parallels the growth of grace in our souls and the growth of Christianity. By our paying attention and following Jesus's teachings and the Holy Spirit's inspirations, more and more obstacles are removed from our own souls; this allows more space for God to occupy, to expand his kingdom in our souls. And as we become more "Christianized" by God's influence in our souls, the more we attract others; they are more interested and inclined to convert, to give their lives to follow Christ like we have done.

The parable of the woman and the yeast, as told in Matthew 13:33, is another example that Jesus used to explain in simple stories the tremendous mystery of spreading God's love for us and, at the same time, spreading this love to the "ends of the earth."

This is our life's work: to remove all that is not of God from our lives in order that God can come more and more effectively in our souls. God is the gentle ruler. He will not push his way into our souls; he waits at the door of our hearts to let him in. The goal of our religion is to have God totally occupy all areas of our souls. This protecting of our souls from losing God through our sins and the continuing to fill our lives with good works never ceases until our last breath. What a great responsibility God has given us; what a great privilege! We give thanks to God for this privilege, and we beg his help and support to do this work well.

1. I will pray often to remember that I am God's kingdom, and I must keep it pure, active, and growing in love for God.

2. I will review my plans for deeper conversion to God, to following Jesus. I will list faults, sins that I most often fall into. I will work at forming new habits.

3. I will continue to read Scripture to gain more understanding and knowledge and love of God, Jesus, and the Holy Spirit.

Notes:

Chapter 36

What and Why Redemption

THE CROSS IS the Christian symbol of our redemption. It is also the Christian symbol of pain, suffering, contradictions. Redemption is defined as making up for something that was lost, a replacing, a ransom. Christian redemption is about Adam's disobedience causing mankind to lose all the supernatural benefits that God had given him when he created Adam and Eve; this caused mankind (us) to lose all the supernatural benefits also. This caused man to be a slave of sin (the devil). God had not intended that we had to endure pain, suffering, and death in this life; Adam's disobedience to God's commandment caused all this havoc, which continues to this day.

Only God could make up for the disobedience. Only God could undo the results of this original sin, which all of Adam's descendants would forever be born with; of course, that includes us. This sin shut heaven for all of us forever; we needed someone to change this for us.

Jesus became man, suffering all that we human beings suffer. His sufferings, especially in his passion and death, freed us from the clutches of the devil and sin. He redeemed us. He was judged in our place. Jesus was our ransom. We now have the opportunity to eternal happiness in heaven.

Jesus's suffering as a human person like us was sufficient to make up for Adam's disobedience. In fact, only one drop of blood from Jesus was sufficient. But Jesus endured his difficult life, from an impoverished birth, his passion and death, to show us and emphasize the love that God the Father has for us, and to emphasize how serious disobedience to God's laws and decrees is to mankind. And Jesus wanted to teach us how to live, avoiding sin.

God also wanted us to help us make up for the sins that we and everyone else constantly continue to commit. God wanted us to share in Christ's sufferings to ransom, free from sin, us and others; disobedience to God's laws and to Jesus's teaching continues rampantly in this twenty-first century. We and others too must be ransomed from unrepented sins to enter heaven; we still depend upon Jesus.

Yes, we Christians can participate in Christ's passion. John Paul II, as quoted in *In Conversation with God*, volume 5, page 392, tells us, "In the spiritual dimension of the work of Redemption he (the suffering person) is serving, like Christ, the salvation of his brothers and sisters. He is carrying out an irreplaceable service... It is suffering, more than anything else, which clears the way for grace which transforms human souls. Suffering, more than anything else, makes present in the history of humanity the power of the Redemption."

We Christians can accept suffering, pain, annoyances, frustrations, difficulties of all kind with calm acceptance because we know the secret that the world does not know. Our Lord allows suffering for our own purification and sanctification. This suffering is like a fire that burns away the rust of our failures, omissions, sins, and therefore, cleanses our souls. Not only is this great gift for us, but the Lord uses our suffering for others, especially our loved ones, and for the whole church, the whole world. How does God do this? That is a mystery!

Suffering can be very beneficial as it can cause us to turn to the Lord more intensely, more frequently, more hopefully; we can become more aware of the need of seeking his divine mercy. In the Old Testament, the prophet Hosea, in chapter 6, verse 1, tells us to come to the Lord for healing: "Come, let us return to the Lord, For it is he who has rent (torn), but he will heal us; he has struck us, but he will bind our wounds."

All the disturbances, distractions, aggravations from other people, along with the pains and sufferings from illnesses, can be great gifts that we give to ourselves and others. These are great gifts if we accept them for the glory and love of God in a totally Christian manner; calmly, joyfully, graciously, humbly, we accept them as Jesus's will for us right now. Josemaría Escrivá, founder of Opus Dei, an organization for laymen and clergy, advocated the truth that everyone is called to holiness and that the ordinary life can lead to sanctity. Escrivá has been reported to have said that only stupidity can cause us to ignore the blessings that we can receive through daily sufferings.

Therefore, we can look at a cross with humble joy and peace; it can serve as a reminder of the great sacrifice that Jesus suffered for us and the treasure that we have in our power to use for our benefit, for the benefit of those we love, benefit for the whole world! We have the awesome power from Jesus to participate in his great redemption; we can make reparation for our sins and the sins of those we love and the sins of the whole world! Thanks be to God!

1. I will offer my sufferings for good intentions. I will try to "treasure" suffering as "good."

2. I will study the Holy Scripture to see how Jesus and other holy people suffered for the holy cause of saving souls.

Notes:

Chapter 37

Christian Necessities

WHEN WE MAKE a firm decision to become a follower of Christ, a Christian, by giving Jesus our life to rule and guide, we call that a "conversion." We can have many conversions throughout our lives because we can give him more and more of our lives every day. We pray that this will be our experience.

We can change our minds in a split second; sadly, we can choose to change our lives to leave Jesus and pursue a life of serious sins. That is the reason why we need to stay close to Jesus. The Holy Spirit is always with us to give us his special help with conforming our lives to Jesus. To be a Christian and to remain faithful to Christ, it is important that we practice the virtues that Jesus emulated; the Holy Spirt is the teacher and guide in helping us achieve a virtuous life by giving us his gifts and fruits. Scripture lists these gifts and fruits of the spirit. We look at the list of seven spiritual gifts: wisdom, understanding, counsel, fortitude, knowledge, piety, fear of the Lord. One list of nine fruits of the Holy Spirit includes love, joy, peace, patience, kindness, goodness, gentleness, faithfulness, and self-control. We will study a few of these today as a good start.

One of the virtues we practice is the *fear of the Lord*. No! No! This is not just being afraid of the punishing, stern, strict judge, but the *fear of offending our Father, who loves us so much!* It is true that it is not unwise to fear the punishment of the consequences of our sins, and that is often what we Christians have when we first begin our following of Jesus. But then, we learn to know and love God; we become more afraid of hurting or disappointing him. That is a more complete and realistic reason for fear. In Jeramiah 31:3, the Lord God tells us, "I have loved you with an everlasting love"; and Jesus tells us in John 15:15, "I have called you my friends." Yes, God is our lover! This virtue helps us want to stop offending God by our sins, faults, imperfections because he loves us so much. (The world, the devil, tries to trick us; they do not want us to know how much God loves us.)

Another virtue we need to help us on our path to God is the virtue of *fortitude*. Because of our human weaknesses, we need help to keep us from falling into sin, which we do over and over and over. This virtue gives us the courage and the strength from God to continue bravely the struggle to succeed in following Jesus. Our own strength and courage "ebbs and flows," like the tide, with our moods, feelings, circumstances; but when we exercise any effort, the Holy Spirit rushes with his help to add to our efforts. He does this "time and time and time again," as often as we fall and rise again. A great sin is not rising again, not starting over because we believe we are too stupid, weak, and that surely God has given up on us! He never gives up looking, seeking us. Jesus loves our daily effort, not necessarily the results!

The virtue of *prudence* informs us, teaches us, how to reach our goal: knowing, loving, serving God by following Jesus Christ. The Holy Spirit, with our effort, teaches us what we need to do and how to do this in order to reach our goal. Prudence is a virtue that helps us to make schedules, wise plans, reachable goals. It helps our "common sense" make spiritual decisions to follow Jesus. (This differs from strictly worldly prudence, which may use any means to achieve the goal, even sinful means.)

Diligence is the partner of prudence to move us along on our journey to God, following Jesus. Diligence is doing all that we do well, the best that we can at this time. We need to struggle against laziness and sloppiness and disinterest in our activities and in doing our duties, both in strictly spiritual affairs and in our worldly affairs. We can elevate to the level of spiritually beneficial all these duties, jobs, activities, no matter how we feel, when we follow Jesus. Diligence makes us observe opportunities to do good. Diligence is what makes us responsible in keeping our lives and our goals on schedules, routines, or rules of life, which prudence has helped us to make. This virtue keeps us from acting on our moods or whims which is one of the devil's most effective tactics for tricking us; he knows how to attack us in our own weaknesses of character. (It is the small things that we do all day long for God, the way Jesus teaches us, that are the greatest good for our souls.)

Acquiring the virtue of *patience* allows us to live peacefully, generously at all times, good or bad, easy or difficult. Patience is accepting all, everything and everyone, that come into our lives, because we know that all are allowed or provided for by God for our benefit or the benefit of others. Our spiritual well-being and the well-being of others are God's greatest concerns. In this lifetime, we may never see or know the reasons for many of the happenings in our life. By keeping our eyes on Jesus and following the Holy Spirit's instructions and inspirations, we will be able to accept everything that is unpleasant or pleasant, hurtful or beneficial, difficult or not, with more ease because of the love of God, whom we know loves us; and he asks us to trust him in all situations.

The root of all the virtues is *humility*; it is the "mother lode." Without humility, we cannot love God or anyone else. As Christians, as followers of Jesus, our lives here on earth are to promote glory to God, to know, love, and serve him who created us. Jesus's whole life was to give glory to God by fulfilling God's will; he did fulfill all that God had sent him to do on earth. We must do this also. We must do what God has willed for us, not what we decide to do; in other words, we do God's will, not ours.

Too often, we forget that by ourselves, we are "nothing," made from "nothing." God elevated us; he made us his children by grace, brothers to Jesus, and members of his church, the body of Christ. When we "glory" in ourselves, our accomplishments, our self-satisfactions, our talents, we fail miserably as Christians. Our world promotes the elevation of "self," puffed-up self-esteem, complacency with who we "think" we are; the results are clearly seen in the arrogance, the pridefulness, the self-satisfaction of so many of us. We must remember often what we hear, especially at the beginning of the Lenten season: "Remember, man, that thou art dust and to dust you will return."

The study and practice of all the virtues, gifts, and fruits of the Holy Spirit are the *work of our entire lives. It will finish with our last breath.* This is the work of the Christian warrior, the faithful Christian, the beloved child of God! We learn that acquiring these virtues helps us to serve others better. The virtues and gifts and talents that we have are not for us alone; all these are for the benefit and betterment of all others, those close to us and those in the world we live in.

1. I will make a study of all the gifts and fruits of the spirit; I will evaluate myself often, making resolutions, plans, as necessary to acquire the virtues. These may already be the plans I have made.

2. I will study Scripture, especially that which concerns the gifts and fruits of the Holy Spirit: 1 Corinthians 12; Romans 12; Ephesians 4:1; 1 Peter 4.

Notes:

Chapter 38

Keepers of Peace

PEACE AND JOY are what we twenty-first-century Christians must bring to the world. Fear, anxiety, confusion reign everywhere, in the world, in our country, in our cities and towns, in our neighborhood, and sadly, in many of our homes. Christian apathy and indifference and sloth have been a major reason why we are losing our Christian culture of "peace to and among men." Let us look at what Scripture tells us about peace for ourselves and for others.

For those of us who desire and strive to be Jesus's disciples today, the message is the same as that which Jesus gave those frightened disciples over two thousand years ago: "Be not afraid; it is I." And Matthew 28:20 records Jesus saying, "I will be with you until the end of the world."

When Jesus first appeared to the huddled, frightened disciples in Jerusalem after his crucifixion and resurrection form the dead, his first words to them were, "Peace be with you," according to Luke 23:36–43.

The disciples were afraid; they feared that the Jews who were responsible for Jesus's death would be searching for them because they were followers of Jesus. They were afraid to be killed too. Then when he suddenly appeared in their midst, they thought he was a ghost. He showed them his wounds so that they could recognize him as the one who was crucified. Then to further prove that he was not a ghost, he asked for food, took it, and ate it. They believed; they were filled with joy and peace!

The pope Saint John Paul II said that there two kinds of peace. One kind is the peace we work hard to attain for ourselves. We struggle to succeed in worldly activities; we seek for security, well-being, pleasure, and other worldly goals that we believe we can achieve on our own. This kind of peace is fragile and insecure; so much can happen to destroy this self-made happiness: illness, financial changes, loss of love ones, and pandemics. This peace is not to be trusted because things beyond our control often do happen; therefore, we can have much fear always on the alert.

The other peace that we Christians seek is not based on our own independent work, our self-made peace. We Christians believe that true and lasting peace comes from God and from being faithful to his laws. Psalm 119:165 says it well: "Lovers of your teachings have much peace; for them there is no stumbling block."

Because we know that God is our loving Father, that everything is designed by him for our greatest good, we can "relax" in our living and working hard in this "crazy" world. We will experience hard and difficult times for ourselves and our loved ones. We will experience some fear and anxiety, but our "bottom-line" peace will remain because this peace is based on our knowing we are God's children, and God is "taking care of all the details." We work like everyone else, but we know that God is the "real doer" in all endeavors because we have given all of our lives and all activities to him.

This peace built on the strong foundation of "knowing, loving, and serving God" is the best way to achieve the lasting peace that we can give to the world. This peace, only given by God, gives courage and direction, not only for those who live with and around us, but to the whole world as it spreads. When we Christians live the "peace and joy" of our lives as sons and daughters of the living God, the brother and close friend of Jesus, we are like small stones thrown into the pond of our little existence. The stones, our lives, cause waves and waves, circles and circles around us, circles of peace; this peace spreads.

No one of us Christians can say, "There is nothing I can do about this violent world." There is something all of us can do: we can follow Jesus closely, convert our lives in the areas that need conversion, do all we do for the intentions of peace and joy for the world.

God gives us joy and peace even in the most troubling times, like that which the world is experiencing today. When we have found this treasure, he will automatically spread it!

1. I want to be known as a peaceful, joyful person. I can amend my life in the areas that I need to amend, like practicing more trust in God and so on.

2. Frequent examination of conscience will give the Holy Spirit the opportunity to show me what and how to change.

3. Using the plans I have already made during these days of "lessons," or starting to make plans, I will put into action all I can to make myself and my world more peaceful, trusting, in the Lord.

Notes:

Chapter 39

Jesus Is the Final Word

AT THE END of our *first* study of the lessons, we review the plan God had for the world after creation when his plan was ruptured by Adan's sin. The plan is Jesus, the one who was, the one who is, and the one who will be forever. Jesus is the final answer; he embodies all we need to know and all we need to follow to get back home to God, who created us and awaits us.

Jesus tells us, boldly and frankly, with no apologies or hesitation, in Matthew 24:35 and Mark 13:21 that all, everything, will disappear at the end of time; he says that both heaven and earth will vanish, but his Words will never pass away. These words are addressed to us; what Jesus said when he lived on earth was, and is, truth now and forever. How reassuring this is for us, who often do not know who or what to believe. We are constantly faced with big and little decisions and choices daily; we may get confused with a barrage of advice and guides.

We Christians have the "game plan"; Jesus is the map for our entire lives, planned by the loving God, who created us because he loves us. He planted us in our mothers' wombs, and then he sent us from our mothers' wombs into the world with his instructions on how to live, in the time and place where we are. We are to work at knowing, loving, serving him; and this will ensure our peace and joy now and forever. There is a stipulation: *we must know, love, and serve others: and we learn this by following Jesus.* The answer to the fulfillment of the purpose of our life is Jesus.

We twenty-first-century citizens of the world are sophisticated in the use of instruments of communication—worldly, pleasurable, sensual, useless events. Too often, for most of us, we do not use this information to accomplish God's plan for us. Unfortunately, this wave of constant information results only in "filling our time" with useless information and amusements; too much precious time is wasted because these things do not advance our relationship with Jesus, who is the answer to all our questions, our seeking for happiness, fulfillment, peace, and joy.

Sadly, too many of us Christians do not utilize the information that God has provided in Scripture, both the Old and the New Testament of the Holy Bible, information on God's plan of salvation for us after Adam and Eve's sin of disobedience. We do not "see" the Old Testament history of God getting the world ready for Jesus, the Messiah. Nor do we understand Jesus as God's great gift, revealed in the New Testament.

The necessary quiet reading, studying, and meditating on God's speaking to and instructing us in Scripture is lost in the noise and deluge of information that is poured out constantly. Our souls are filled with the things, ideas, pleasures, amusements of the world, which is rapidly sliding into the grave of "death" without God. True, we now have available a great many sources from which to get information *about* God and Jesus and the church; some very good information is at our fingertips. (Some serious distortions and much erroneous information are also plentiful; we must be careful to distinguish.)

Sadly, however, all this information is just "head stuff"; our hearts must be involved. We must *know and love a person*. We must have an intimate relationship with Jesus; our prayers, our meditation on his life and his words, will bring about a close friendship with him. We will get to really know him; we will experience his presence in our lives.

The Holy Bible is the love story of God for his people. In the Old Testament, the whole history, events, and the prophets, kings, saintly and evil people are all God's recording for us to listen to, internalize the love message, and see his preparation for the coming of the Messiah, God himself in the form of a man. The New Testament, starting with Mary's fiat and Jesus's birth, is a fulfilling and completing of God's *love letter* to us. His *letter* to us continues daily in all the people, events, natural events, our surroundings—all are messages to us. *Jesus is the love letter, the love messages, the text messages.*

Sadly, too many of us, men and women, Christians and not, are uninterested. We say, "We don't need a God or his church, his religion, to tell us what to do or not do. We are capable of taking care of ourselves. We don't know this Christian God and don't want to. We don't care. We are fine with our own god." Too many are missing the most important person in their lives, the *Christian, the Christ, Jesus.*

We who know that we need God, who knows our dependence on him, are overwhelmed with gratitude that Jesus did come as our Messiah, our Savior and Redeemer! And we give thanks for his remaining with us "until the end of our time," watching and caring for us, especially through the Holy Spirit.

Jesus has come, has finalized God's commandments and laws; Jesus has taught us how to live, how to love, how to trust, and even how to die. Jesus has taught us that he and the Father will live with us now if we follow his commandments. We find some of his loving words in John 14:15.

There we have it! The instructions, the answer to the purpose of our lives: to know, love, serve God, and be happy forever with him. Jesus has and is the plan, the map, the GPS coordinates. This gift is given to us, was given to all generations before us, and will be given to all generations that will come after us! We must help! We must give them this gift, this Jesus!

The *end* of our lessons will be with our last breath. Until then, we begin again, we review, we fall, and we rise again; we start over and over. That is God's plan for us. Jesus is "our way, our truth, our very life." "Come, Lord Jesus!"

Notes:

Chapter 40

Reviewing Our Choice: Life or Death

GOD CREATED EACH one of us; he loved us into being in this time and place. He created us in the way he imagined each of us; to look the way we look, to have these personalities and temperaments; to be children of our own parents who helped him in our creations. Nothing was accidental. And God created each one of us for a particular purpose.

God gave us free will, the freedom to make many choices; the most important choice of our entire life is always before us; it is a choice which we make moment by moment. The choice is to fulfill God's purpose for our lives, the reason for which God created us, or to ignore him and determine our own purposes.

Let us review that which is important and essential in making our eternal choice: to choose life for God, ending in eternal happiness; or to choose death, a life ignoring God, ending in eternal suffering. God created us to be happy with him forever in heaven. God created us to know him, love him, and serve him here on earth. This requires much work and some suffering on our part. (This was not the original plan; because our first parents sinned, they lost the supernatural gifts which we would have inherited from them; we would have known, loved, and served God easily and joyfully.) With or without God, as Scripture tells us, life is filled with troubles and sorrows; but when we live for and work with God, we live in peace, much joy, and gain an eternal reward.

We fulfill God's purpose for our lives: to know him, to love him, to serve him, and to be happy with him in heaven by following Jesus. Jesus tells us that he is the way, the truth, the life; no one comes to the Father except through him. Jesus came into the world to prove his and the Father's divinity and their characteristics of love and mercy.

1. Jesus established a church to give nourishment, graces, guidance, and support to aid us for our entire lives. He has told us that he would not leave us orphaned when he ascended into heaven; he did not. Jesus gave us his church and the Holy Spirit to guide the church and to guide each one of us personally also.

2. The lessons that we must master and put into practice will require focus and effort until we breathe our last breath. This will require spending our entire life cultivating and improving our relationship with Jesus through prayer and living according to his teachings. Therefore, we pray, "Come, Lord Jesus!" And we begin again and again, to review, to learn, to relearn, to put into practice his teachings.

About the Author

YVONNE ARDOIN DARDEAU has a BA in Education, an MS in Rehabilitation Counseling Education, and is Reality Therapy Certified. She taught high school, technical school, and special education students. She was a rehabilitation counselor in a hospital cardiac unit; she worked as counselor and director in substance abuse centers. She is now retired from teaching and counseling, but she is now writing a monthly newspaper column and working on writing books to encourage Christians to faithfully follow Jesus to survive and to help convert this near-pagan twenty-first century. The author is blessed with 4 adult children and their spouses, has 9 grandchildren and some spouses, 3 great-grandchildren, 4 sisters and their families. She lives in Ville Platte, a small town in rural south-central Louisiana, Cajun country of French descendants!

CPSIA information can be obtained
at www.ICGtesting.com
Printed in the USA
BVHW081603290421
606131BV00001B/73